C000214618

THE
WESTERN MYSTERY
TRADITION

THE
WESTERN MYSTERY
TRADITION

The Esoteric Heritage of the West

Christine Hartley

Introduction by Alan Richardson

THOTH PUBLICATIONS
Loughborough, Leicestershire

This edition 2003

Copyright © The Estate of Christine Hartley 1986
Introduction © Alan Richardson 2003

All rights reserved. No reproduction, copy or transmission of
this publication may be made without written permission.
No paragraph of this publication may be reproduced, copied or
transmitted save with written permission or in accordance with
the provision of the Copyright Act 1956 (as amended).
Any person who does any unauthorised act in relation to this
publication may be liable to criminal prosecution and civil
claims for damages.

The Moral Rights of the Author have been asserted.

A CIP catalogue record for this book is available from the
British Library.

Cover design by Bob Eames

ISBN 1 870450 24 8

Printed and bound in Great Britain

Published by Thoth Publications
64, Leopold Street, Loughborough, LE11 5DN
web address: www.thoth.co.uk
e-mail: orders@thoth.co.uk

Contents

Introduction

Christine Hartley died on 29 September 1985. This was Michaelmas Day, the day of St Michael and all the Angels. It was an appropriate time to go for someone who had been so closely involved with the deva kingdoms. For the past few years she had been sorely troubled with the blindness of cataracts, the diabetes of extreme age, and occasional falls. Refusing to enter any sort of old people's home she maintained her self-sufficiency until the last by taking a flat in warden-supervised accommodation on Hyde Street, Winchester. With the exception of thrice-weekly visits from a home help she looked after herself and got on as best she could. She was still writing up until the last few weeks of her life. Fiercely independent, there was not a shred of self-pity or complaint in her. When her death came it was a relief; and its anticipation held not the slightest fear. She was 88 years old and exceedingly glad to go.

Quite apart from her magical background her life had been a notable one. Shortly after the Great War she formed her own literary agency under her maiden name of Christine Campbell Thomson. Since then she came to know, with varying degrees of intimacy, many of the major literary figures of this century. She wrote a great number of books herself, including several lightweight romances under the name of Dair Alexander, as well as editing a series of anthologies of horror and supernatural stories, plus the very first 'Good Loo Guide' and a book of Children's Names. Nowhere do we get the slightest hint that she herself was steeped in occult knowledge; that as a fully-trained initiate of the Golden Dawn she was, at her height, a formidable priestess indeed. with the talent to take her consciousness into other realms.

Her first contact with the outer court of the magical world was via the novelist J. W. Brodie-Innes, who had tried to persuade her

to join an 'occult group' that he knew about, for which he felt she
would be well suited. This, of course, was the Hermetic Order of
the Golden Dawn. She refused, however, because although she
was quite aware of her own feyness, she had (as she put it) other
things to do. Ten years later she became the pupil of a woman
whom Brodie-Innes had himself initiated, namely Violet Firth, who
was rather better known even then as 'Dion Fortune'.

It was within Dion's Fraternity of the Inner Light that she came
to work with one of the senior adepti, Charles Richard Foster
Seymour, known by his Motto as *Foy Pour Devoir*, or F.P.D.
Everyone called him *Colonel* Seymour. His few intimates knew
him as 'Kim'. Their relationship as priest and priestess began in
July 1937 and never really ended, even though Seymour died six
years later. She was his shakti. She also worked magic with
Anthony Daw and Edward Maltby, both military men who (with
Seymour) belonged to a branch of British Intelligence that was
actively directed toward the occult threat posed by magicians within
the Nazi hierarchy. (Interestingly, Cecil Williamson, one of the
founder figures of modern Wicca, also worked in the same
department under Major Maltby, who was married to Dion
Fortune's sister-in-law. The full story of the British government's
occult war against the Third Reich has still to be told.)

The magical partnership between Christine Hartley and Kim
Seymour has been told in some detail in my book *Dancers to the
Gods*, and in my biography of Dion Fortune, *Priestess*. The former,
containing some of their Magical Diaries, suggested that the current
which they had channelled had been disrupted by the War, but that
it had in some way been renewed quite recently, helped in part by
the very nature of Christine's longevity. The latter, being a biography
of Dion herself, showed how Seymour and Hartley used a different
set of inner contacts to those within the mainstream of the Inner
Light.

But let us be very careful here. Let us not fall prey to
psychobabble. In plain terms these people believed themselves in
direct psychic contact with discarnate beings of a high order. These
beings were the Secret Chiefs, as they were called then. Crudely
speaking they were like Spirit Guides but on a considerably higher
level. They should not be 'explained' with modern jargon about
archetypes, repressed complexes and the like, for if we do so we

fail completely to understand the essence of what these people experienced and believed. And if we regard the likes of Seymour and Hartley as unlearned, unsophisticated wretches with no understanding of the vagaries of human consciousness, then we will lose something very precious in our own lives: we will lose access to the Otherworld, our humanity.

Since the scandals about Madame Blavatsky, Mathers, and all the many types of nonsense perpetrated by Mrs Besant and Charles Leadbeater, magicians have kept very quiet about this whole concept of Secret Chiefs, or Inner Plane Adepti, as Dion came to call them. Many of the reasons for such secrecy were sound; others were not. At any rate they kept very quiet, or else invoked words from the dread regions of psychology to make it all sound respectable. Carl Jung did this, as new research has shown. He used apparently scientific terminologies to hide from his sponsors, patrons and patients the fact that he was communing with spirits. Literally. So whether these Secret Chiefs really were (and are) discarnate entities or merely neurons firing in the brain is not that important because to the magicians, the universe behaved as though these contacts were real. And the simple fact is, they are.

So listen, and accept it : Seymour and Hartley were in direct mind-to-mind contact with beings from other dimensions who had, and have, an evolutionary interest in our humanity.

In fact Seymour and Hartley were in touch with a variety of these Otherworld beings, as their Diaries make clear. In particular they were close to Kha'm-uast and Ne Nefer Ka Ptah, who were historical characters from the reign of Rameses II. There was also Lord Eldon, who had been Chancellor of England, and Cleomenes III, a Spartan King murdered upon a Tau cross, from whose body, legends said, a great dragon crawled.

Dion Fortune touched upon at least some of these contacts to some degree. For a few years the Colonel and his especial pupils co-existed quite happily with her - she at 3 Queensborough Terrace, they next door at number 2. Around 1938, however, a sense of strain developed between them to such an extent that Seymour left, joining a Golden Dawn temple which had been limping along under the leadership of Dr W. E. Carnegie Dickson. In due course, CCT, as they all called her, came to join him.

Christine would never tell me the name of this temple, although she let me have some of the fragments of records which have survived. However, judging from her comments that she had known R. W. Felkin, and had often worked with the sister temple, the Hermes, in Bristol, I would judge it to have been the Merlin Temple of the Stella Matutina, as run from Carnegie Dickson's rooms in Upper Harley Street and also Culford Park, although others have argued that it nmight have been the old Amoun Temple given a new lease of life.

Once, I asked her if there was any contact that was dominant in her life beyond all others, under whose aegis she particularly worked. She replied, without hesitation, 'Merlin'.

Whatever the name, the temple was in a dire state when Seymour joined it. He brought in new blood and worked hard at building up the group mind. From the scanty records it is clear that they brought through much in the way of what seemed 'far memories', and made contact with the immediate Secret Chiefs of this particular lodge. There is a working dated 7 November 1942 which reads as follows:

> Working for the first time with the Order method on the triangle. Went through to the volcanic region and met the guide who was M. With him we went over the road which appeared to be glass over fire, and in front over the hilltops was a vast Sun: our guide typified Astral Fire. We went up the hill and then the scene changed and I found myself in the inner room... They had taken away the long table and put up an altar at the far end, in front of which was S.R.M.D. (Mathers), B(rodie) I(nnes) and F.M., the first of the three being in tremendously bright robes. Accompanied by the guide, who walked between us, we went up to the altar. In front of S.R.M.D. was a shaft of light with the Dove and the Cup illumined in it. Lines of power ran between the six of us and we formed the two interlaced triangles, our guide being the lowest point and S.R.M.D. the upper one. The lines of power were first gold and then changed to blue and red. An aura like a rainbow was built over the six of us completely enclosing us and the power and peace were very great. Then we returned by the usual route and through the triangle.

I do not know who F.M. was, but the guide was surely Merlin.

Seymour died in 1943, but not before he and CCT had been granted admission to Co-Masonry. It was this movement that

was to prove the enduring passion of his priestess's life. Up until
the end she still managed to attend lodge meetings in Portsmouth.

Shortly after the war she married again (her first marriage, to
Oscar Cook, had ended in divorce). Her second husband was
Henry Alexander Hartley, an electrical engineer with a shrewd
knowledge of occultism in general and astrology in particular. They
also shared a contact that had come to loom increasingly large in
their lives. This was the wizard-sage Michael Scot, one of whose
graves can be found in Melrose Abbey. They celebrated their
own mystic marriage over Scot's tomb before ratifying it in the
more accepted sense.

I first met Christine in the late 70's, although I had corresponded
with her for some time before that, as we shared a passion for the
little-known beauties and mysteries of the Northumbrian landscape.
She and her husband had almost bought a farm up near Otterburn,
and I had written to her a lot about the (then) almost unknown host
of circles and standing stones in that area - especially the
Threestoneburn Circle in the north of the county. When she came
to the door of her beautiful house, 'West Wing', in the village of
Exton, it was obvious that this small woman was a very formidable
presence. You knew, in fact, that here was a real priestess, and
that her teachings were often imparted at levels that went far
beyond mere intellect. You couldn't help but be aware that whatever
lay behind her was exceedingly active in touching you at subliminal
levels.

When she came to write *The Western Mystery Tradition* she
was 71 years old, and somewhat perturbed by a modern culture
which was increasingly turning its young face eastward for spiritual
inspiration. While not detracting from the value of eastern
philosophies she was insistent that Britain had its own mystery
tradition, one that was hidden in myth and legend, and in the land
itself - a tradition that was every bit as profound, holy, and potent
as anything beyond our shores. More importantly, by nature of
our birthright, it was available to us here and now, within ourselves.
She who had known Merlin on the inner planes, and been with him
to the Celtic Otherworld in her Body of Light, was more than
happy to show us the entrance to this realm. It was not a path of
worship, but of Work.

The Western Mystery Tradition can be read with enjoyment by anyone who has no notion of, or is sceptical toward, this whole background. It is a book that is dense with information and occasionally makes demanding reading; it is laced with magical hints and enlivened by personal comments, and there are places where you have to read between the lines and below the Moon to touch its energies. Parts of it were written in full trance in a New York hotel room, under the direct control of the Colonel. Parts of it seem to contain a message, but hidden away behind a thicket of imagery designed to conceal as much as reveal. Behind it all there is literary skill, scholarship, poignance, and a real vision. In an era when the few magicians around were all busy apologizing for their craft, and the young generations were looking toward the Himalayas, it was one of the few books to keep the flame of the West alight. At the time, it was largely ignored.

Now, with magic resurgent against all odds and logic, we can appreciate it rather more: not merely as a collection of dry words and themes but as Christine intended in the first place: as a treasure house of images.

The treasure is ours by right. All we must do now is use it wisely.

Alan Richardson

Dedication

For
F.P.D. and D.N.F.
In Saecula Saeculorum
Shatter the lamp; the light remains

Preface

This is an attempt to present to the reader the story of the great heritage to which we, as members of the West, have access. It is not to be taken as exhaustive, as scholarly or as being in any sense the last word on the subject; but it is intended to be an exposition of the Western Tradition and Teaching so that those who are interested may see that their own Mysteries are as worthy of consideration and reverence as those of any other Tradition; neglected and uncultivated as they may have been for hundreds of years, yet still they flourish secretly in the hearts of the few. The corn is still green and the ears are ripening for the harvest.

There is no bibliography attached to this book; when one begins to search out the traditions, the same stories, the same allusions occur over and over again; it would be impossible to say from which actual source a story was obtained. Where quotations have been given in the body of the book the references are made clear.

I would, however, like to give very special thanks to the Warden and Council of the Society of the Inner Light, who have most generously put many papers at my disposal and have given me much help and encouragement.

The last two chapters of this work are based on unpublished notes and talks by F.P.D., which have served as aides-memoire to the years of instruction he gave to me and to many others. I am confident that he approves the use I have made of his teachings.

Christine Hartley
London, 1967

Chapter 1

The Origin of our heritage

I t is highly probable that the first question a reader will ask himself on picking up this book are: Why should there be a book on the Western Mystery Tradition? What is it? Whence does it come? What is its place in the world to-day?

The time has come, it seems, when such a book should be written – a book which cannot of itself be exhaustive but which can at least offer an approach to various aspects of our own background and present a picture of the tapestry which has been woven throughout the ages as a background to our way of life and thought. The Western tradition is the basis of the Western religious feeling, the foundation of our spiritual life, the matrix of our religious formulae, whether we are aware of it or not. To it we owe the life and force of our spiritual world; Christianity was grafted on to it but it is older far than any Christian Church; it is, as will be shown, drawn from the beginning of time.

During the last century there has been a remarkable revival of interest in the meaning and interpretation of religion by means of numerous societies, secret or otherwise. One of the largest and best known is the Theosophical Society, which numbers thousands of people among its members, a large proportion of whom are of the Western races. But many of these societies have derived their knowledge and their spiritual aspirations from the East. That they have by their teachings brought new light and new understanding to thousands of people who have seen in the Oriental esoteric teaching the answer to many of their problems, no one would deny, but one is entitled to ask if by reason of its very nature it is really suitable for Western minds and Western conditions.

The Eastern tradition is developed and intended for the demands of an Oriental life. The East has a far more slowly moving development than the West; its rhythm is different. Let us take as an example the two great Opposites which offer themselves in all forms of progress – the great principles of Force and Form. Broadly speaking the East represents Force and the West Form. The Eastern mystic is content to sit, to meditate and to contemplate; the Western religious is out and about and doing, an active Order. In the less highly developed sections of society the Easterner fritters his time away in inactive beautiful thoughts that fall upon the air and are quite unproductive. The Westerner is apt to go on so many Committees and serve so many good Causes that in the end little but talk may be accomplished.

This, of course, is taking it at its lowest common denominator, but there it is. The physical circumstances, the climatic conditions, the type of food required are all different. And if the Eastern esoteric system is to be practised by Westerners it needs to be very carefully considered and fully understood or the practitioner will by very virtue of his upbringing and background lapse into 'muzzy mysticism' and a repetition of 'beautiful thoughts' which will not help him very far along the path of development.

Moreover, why should we go to the East for our tradition and our mysteries when we have those of our own which are so impeccable in origin and as worthy of consideration, as efficacious in practice as those of any other system in the world?

One might say that the Dark Night of the West took place in the two hundred odd years of gross materialism when the advent of the Hanoverian Kings, however advisable or essential politically, removed from this country its romance and its beauty and plunged it for the time being into a welter of material success, of material outlook, of 'Sunday' religion and a determination to achieve rank and fortune, not necessarily always by the most honourable means. When a man's virtue is measured by his bank balance and his financial stability, a poor but honest thinker has little to recommend him in the eyes of the general public; Art and Poetry and Music and Ritual are despised by the majority and the way of all flesh becomes not the road to ruin but to a mansion in South Kensington. Then you have the nadir of the group soul.

As always happens in such periods of darkness, the mysteries went into abeyance. That their secrets were kept in the hearts of the little band of the faithful goes without saying, since there must always be the repository from which the future generations can draw. But it was not until about the end of the nineteenth century that the uprush of small esoteric and secret societies really began to flourish. After the long night, the new dawn was breaking; the seeds, so long in the darkness of the earth, were germinating and tender, delicate shoots were beginning to raise their heads above the dead or dying earth, to push aside the clods of materialism and demand, with great faith and little knowledge, that the new day-spring should break in the sky. The rise of the Spiritualists, the Christian Scientists, the Co-Masonic Order, the countless groups and societies, many of which have not found their way into the books of reference since they were too small and too secret and in many cases too ephemeral, are all proof that the soul of the country was re-awakening.

The East has always had a spiritual and a romantic call to many – both to the wise and to the foolish. It has been the land of hidden treasure – the Glorious East – the Land of the Sun – and it was natural that those who were desirous of bringing the hidden wisdom once more into their own lives and into the lives of others should turn their eyes in that direction, since there it seemed that the Fire had never been quenched. They did not realize that in doing so they were not only bringing in the new light but they were in one sense denying their own birthright, for behind them lay a tradition as old and as well established as that of any other in the world and since it was their own from time immemorial, it was but waiting for the hour when it should be fanned to life again.

So hungry and thirsty was this land for righteousness that it drank so deeply from the Eastern stream that when a few who knew the eternal privileges of their birthright began to put forward its claims, they found themselves cold-shouldered, crowded out and despised and rejected by their fellow men. What could Britain give to the new regeneration of man? Was she not the symbol of worldly wealth and gross materialism – a nation of shop-keepers? Only in the refined spiritual atmosphere of the East could the true knowledge be found. In the East, with its disregard for material comfort and success with, may it be whispered, its dirt, its inefficiency and its immense ignorance of so much, lay the only road to spiritual development.

St Thomas Aquinas says that the sources of knowledge are two – reason and revelation, and it is by a judicious mixture of these two that one is enabled to learn the secret history of a race.

Nothing that is utterly one-sided can be ultimately successful for it will lack balance. 'East is East and West is West, And never the twain shall meet' may be true on the material and even on the mental plane but it is not necessarily true on the inner planes of which we are thinking. Two parallel lines cannot join, so we were taught some years ago, but higher mathematics are changing that axiom. On the material plane they may run side by side, and, each charged with its own type of energy, give from one to the other by force of magnetism, balanced and perpetually interchanging and interplaying so that the fine line which lies between them is animated by the power of the East and the power of the West till force and form are combined in one harmonious whole.

That there are very close ties between the two systems can be shown by one simple instance. The sign of the triple lines which in India is called *Tri-Sul*. This is itself a Welsh word, and the Sign in the West means the Sacred Dove, the symbol of the Ineffable Name. In the diadem of Wales it becomes the Three Feathers and the true translation of the motto is not *Ich Dien*, I serve, but *Eich Dyn* or Virile Power – the Power of the Spirit of God in Man. The Sign should properly be made within a circle, and it is said that this is indeed the Mark of Cain – the mark not of the criminal but of a man set apart, of such sanctity that no one dared harm him.

But unless the ancient mystery teaching of the West is understood and appreciated it cannot give of its spiritual value. That which is dormant cannot give life until it is itself revivified. The embers can be awakened but the glow must be contacted before the new brand is set alight.

I hope that I shall not be misunderstood when I say that in my own opinion the cobbler should stick to his last; the Westerner, born into this civilization, should study its mysteries and its lore, since they are his birthright. Ignorance of the teaching of other Wisdoms is never to be encouraged or applauded, since in the end all the Gods are one God, but while a man may appreciate and admire the aspects of the one Wisdom exemplified in the philosophies and mysteries of other countries and other channels of evolution, he should surely rest securely and steadily upon the foothold that has been given him in his incarnation into whatever group has been selected for his development. Otherwise he must to some extent be betraying his trust and neglecting the work which he has to do in assisting in the evolution of his own race and the country which gave him birth, and to which, for one lifetime at least, he owes his fullest allegiance. To discard the unsatisfactory, the backward, the uninterested is easy but surely not the line of true progress? If one has had one's own spiritual values awakened, surely it is one's duty to promulgate and propagate them among those with whom one has been instructed to spend at least one lifetime? Otherwise, why be awakened?

It is the evolution of mankind in particular and of the world in general with which we are concerned and not our own spiritual development. We are to be as shining lights in the darkness of materialism, small and wavering no doubt, but still alight. To light our wicks by the oil of alien esoteric teaching cannot encourage our fellow countrymen to place their tapers in our flame; let them recognize the source of our spark as one in which they have a right to share and indeed a duty to pass on, not something which has been brought and learnt from afar and handed out as the only form of spiritual life to be truly alive.

That great teacher and priestess of the Western Mysteries, the late Dion Fortune, whose pupil I was privileged to be, wrote in her book, *Avalon of the Heart*:

Do not let it be forgotten that there is a native Mystery Tradition of the race which has its mature aspect in the sun-worship of the Druids and the beautiful fairy-lore of the Celts, its philosophical aspect in the traditions of alchemy and its spiritual aspect in the Hidden Church, of the Holy Grail, the Church behind the Church, not made with hands, eternal in the heavens. All these have their holy places, mounts and pools of initiation, which are part of our spiritual inheritance. Let those who follow the Inner Way study our native tradition, and re-discover and re-sanctify its holy places; let them make pilgrimage thereto at the times when the power descends and spiritual forces are rushing in like the tide up an estuary and 'every common bush afire with God'. Let them keep vigil in the high places when the cosmic tides are flowing, and the Powers of the Unseen are changing guard and the rituals of the Invisible Church are being worked near the earth.

It is indeed a case of 'Seek and ye shall find'. To him who seeks the knowledge of his heritage the doors are opened wide, but he must first be prepared to rap upon them, and to do that he must know where they are situated.

Where then do we begin in the development of the Western Mysteries? There must be a source and a derivation and a tradition or else we are foundering in an alien sea without a lifeline to which to cling. How far back into the mists of time can we take our lifeline?

Later on in this book we shall be covering the mythical legends, the stories, the histories that go to make up the tradition of our inheritance, but for the moment we must deal with the broadest outline so that the stage is set.

According to our tradition our knowledge comes to us from the lost land of Atlantis, from which, we believe, came some of the travellers from the Summer Lands who took possession of these islands in the days before the Kelts or the Iberians appeared. Remember there can be no proof where there is no written record – and even a written record can be a thing of doubtful probity if it has been set down from hearsay and embroidered with symbol and adorned with legend. A record can be twisted and confused and denied by a later generation, even as is the case nowadays with most of the historical beliefs and assumptions of the last few centuries. The aspect of history has been deliberately altered to suit the politics of the time of the historian; we know, for instance, that Shakespeare's Richard III was made into a malignant deformity because the play was written to please the Tudors and the same applies to numerous biographies and histories.

Perhaps we are safer when we deal with tradition, handed down through the generations by word of mouth. The art of story-telling is the art of disguising truth beneath a variety of simple symbols so designed that they may be handed out to both the wise and the simple and he who has the wisdom may see the truth that lies behind the picture which dresses it for the face of the unseeing world. There can be no greater example of this than the Parables of Jesus in the New Testament. The simple illustrations of everyday life conceal profound truths for those who can penetrate the disguise. During the centuries when the stories are handed down, the symbols change but little. Basically they are the same. The stories are embroidered and redecorated until sometimes but little of the original form remains, but to the wise and the discerning the inner meaning is still apparent, for the eternal symbols of the verities never lose their significance. The lock and the key are there; it is the work of the neophyte to fit them together and open the door of Splendid Inheritance.

In an early book called *Esoteric Orders and their Work* Dion Fortune wrote:

> That which derives from our native folk tradition springs up like water from the soil, made alive by the good brown earth and fresh with the breath of herb and tree; it springs, it sparkles. It vitalizes a man's nature because it puts him in touch with the sun-warmed rain-wet earth – his native earth, that his bare feet trod as a child when his soul was open and he still could feel the unseen.
>
> It blows through his soul like the wind on high-places; it drives over him like the waves of the open sea; and his heart leaps to it like the springing leaping flames of the living fire; for by the dust of his fathers he is kin to the elements in his native land, and by the road of his childhood dreams he approaches the Keltic contact.

We talk so much of tradition in our daily life; our schools, our pageantry, our habits – based on tradition as those of few other countries. Yet, when it comes to dealing with the inner life of those traditions, we are so liable to forget that they ever existed.

It is a curious lapse that has come upon us partly through ignorance, partly through the Teutonic Protestantism brought in when the glory of the old Church rituals was swept away; partly, perhaps, due to that curious meiosis which is so prevalent in the British character; a denigrating of our own however proud we may be of it in our secret hearts, until at last that habit has taken such hold of us that we cannot throw it over and it becomes less of a habit than our real self.

It is said in *The Fates of the Princes of Dyfed* by Cenydd Morus:

> There is accessible a compendium, an explanation, a correlation and explicit setting forth of inward laws; the knowledge, the purpose and the discipline out of which all religions draw their origin and which are the heart of all true religion; which proclaim this to be the end of all existence; that which is now human should be made more than human, divine. We may call this Druidism, we may call it Christian and Buddhist; whatever name may be applied to it, it is a trumpet call to the Divine in each of us, the Grand Hai Atton of the Immortals; it is the Dragon War shout of the ages; 'Y Ddraig Goch a Ddyry – Gychwyn!' - 'The Flame-bright Dragon has arisen – Go forward!'

It was John of Salisbury, successor to the great St Bernard of Chartres who wrote in the thirteenth century 'Our time is served by the beneficence of former days, and often knows more than the latter, but not, naturally, because the spirit of our time is the greater, but because it rests upon other powers and upon the ripe wisdom of our fathers.'

This is a wise and profound saying, for it reminds us that we are only privileged by our later appearance in incarnation to have the knowledge of the former days, which we may even once have helped to make, and that there is no virtue, no value in being born perhaps some seven centuries after those words were written: our knowledge is no greater, though it may perhaps be more extensive and in many cases it is probably less because we cannot see the wood for the trees. The demands of our complicated modern existence have clouded the clear-sightedness possessed by our forefathers and we cannot concentrate as they could do. It is difficult for us to grasp the whole picture, now so crowded with detail, both necessary and unnecessary, and to sort out from the mass the relevant and vital properties that go through each phase of development of the whole story.

To us has been given the work that has been done by our fathers but since no man is perfect, to us all come the entanglement of their mistakes, their false starts, their broken hopes, their devious seeking for the light; it is necessary that we should keep their gleam alive and strengthen it to the best of our own ability, discarding the extraneous matter that has accrued through the years, and even remembering with some awe and with some pride, that we ourselves in some former incarnation may have been permitted to contribute to this very thread which we are now following to the heart of the labyrinth and that it is always possible that we are actually continuing our own piece of the pattern without being consciously aware of it. That little corner of the tapestry which we worked hundreds or thousands of years ago may once more be in our hands for further development. That was made by the essential 'I' and now the essential 'I' is all unconsciously engaged upon it once again. To some it is even given to catch glimpses of their past lives and for them it may be plain that they are but carrying on the next few stitches and that they can see and to some extent assess the progress of the work.

What then is the beneficence of our former days and whence is our time served? All seekers after wisdom should and must ask for the foundation on which their quest is built. For us, in the Western Tradition, our clue to the labyrinth takes us back to the days of Great Atlantis, from whose teachings we believe that our Western mysteries derive their sources. There may be many that still disbelieve in the actual physical, material Atlantis of the past, in spite of the references to it in the classics, in spite of the 'evidence' that these can bring. They may decry its existence but they cannot disprove it. They may talk of the geological and geographical formation of the earth through the millions of years which disqualifies in their eyes any possibility of the existence of this great Continent – but scientists have been found wrong before, as history shows time and time again, and they may not be so right as they think, even in this day and age. Each man must believe that which to him seems right. To those of us who are seeking the light by the way of the Mysteries, Atlantis is a natural physical part of the past which is accepted without diffidence or scruple. Too many of the wise ones have been there in the course of their inner working and have brought back too many descriptions for it to be dismissed as a myth or a dream.

Opinions differ, perhaps naturally, as to the extent of that enormous Continent, which we believe consisted of several islands. It is generally assumed that it lay in the Atlantic between where Africa now lies and South America, stretching northwards towards this part of our globe. It must be remembered also that at the time of which we are speaking the contours of none of the countries which we now know were in the least as they are today; that as one country is engulfed, so another raises its head above the surface of the waters since the level of land and water must be preserved.

It is generally accepted by those who accept Atlantis that the peaks of the Azores are all that remain of that once mighty Continent, and of its largest island, known as Ruta. That when it finally sank in that last tremendous eruption these strange peaks were left above the deep water that engulfed all that was best and worst of that great pre-civilization, as we might call it. Here knowledge of an earlier phase of evolution had been brought to such a pitch that it spilled over into misuse. The wheel of evolution demanded a new cycle and a new manifestation, keeping only the tradition of that which had gone before on which the eternal truths might be based.

There is a school of thought which considers that the present day Ireland is a part of old Atlantis, which is supposed to have stretched as far north. These students attribute the troubles and difficulties of Ireland to the fact that she has never been adjusted to the new cycle of evolution. For the purposes of this book, investigation into this theory is not necessary, even if much circumstantial evidence would be forthcoming. Myself, I would not easily subscribe to it. It is, I think, perhaps possible that Ireland is the residue of some outlying island extant at the time of the submersion of Atlantis. It was certainly the seat of some of the earliest of the mystery temples, as we know of them, but I think it is more probable that the teaching was brought there from Atlantis and that colonies or groups of Atlanteans were already well settled, but not that the land itself was a part of the great Continent. There were Atlantean settlements in much of the then known world. It is customary to think of the teaching being brought over by the survivors of the last of the great catastrophes, but actually such knowledge as we may have indicates that there were settlements overseas and that it was these settlements which inculcated and continued the mystery work of the Mother Continent.

Those who held the wisdom of the priests knew what was to come to pass; the upheaval was not unexpected and preparations had been made to deal with it. The wise ones knew in their secret

communings and their ability to read the future what was coming
to their land, and they naturally took precautions to guard and
preserve the secret wisdom of which they were the custodians
throughout eternity, as we understand it.

So from time to time the missionaries went out to spread the
knowledge, establish Mystery Schools and form colonies of the
wisdom. We know that some of them went to Egypt and some
went to what is now Central America and the country of the Mayas,
where they left records in the shape of stones and pyramids and
drawings which are parallel to those which their contemporaries
left in Egypt; others went east and north to found the Hibernian
Schools and to settle in the Scillies. Whatever schools may have
been established during the actual existence of Atlantis, I think we
may reasonably take its fall as the starting point of our own
consideration of the Mystery Traditions of the West.

What was the Wisdom of Atlantis? It is difficult to define it too
closely. It was, so far as we know, polytheistic in the sense that
there were various aspects of the One God, worshipped according
to the focusing point of his power. The great Temple on Ruta was
dedicated to Poseidon, the sea god who is the parent of all other
sea gods – of Neptune and Lir and Manannan – for Atlantis was
of an age when the sea and the gods thereof were in the ascendant.
From the sea, from the great deeps came all life, as we know not
only from the traditional story in the book of Genesis but from the
scientists who have investigated the beginnings of our time, and so
it was that life in the form of the sea god was worshipped during
those long years of the early evolution.

Further on in this book we shall deal with the cycles of the gods
as they are handed down in the legends and the myths of the
Western islands, but for the moment let us stand at the opening of
the door, with the Hibernian Mystery Schools carrying the seeds
of the wisdom inherited from Great Atlantis, from whom we believe
that we derive our own traditions and our own mysteries. And for
those who dwell lovingly – as indeed we all do – upon the great
Temples of Egypt – let them also remember that they too derive
their teaching from Atlantis.

When the final great eruption took place the last of those who
were to be saved took ship from the island and fared northwards.
Imagine for a moment the scene on the reef-encrusted shore of

lost Lyonesse, when the great waves that had overwhelmed the centre of culture and religion of the whole of the known world swept on their storm-tossed crests the little boats that had survived the deluge and brought the last of the survivors to the islands. Priest and priestess, they scrambled ashore on that strange coastline – on the southwest of Ireland, on the lost land of Lyonesse, on the indentured bays of Wales.

And among those who came to rest were two – a priest and a priestess – one of whom was called Merlin and the other Morgan, known later as le Fay. Now, Merlin means simply the man from the sea and Morgan, equally simply, means the woman from the sea and because she was a priestess and skilled in magic art they later called her le Fay or the Fairy, or the Witch.

I need not, I feel sure, remind you that these were generic names and that there have been cycles of Merlins and cycles of Morgans and, indeed, cycles of Arthurs. Difficulty arises when someone such as Malory or Tennyson concentrates a generic hero in one of his latter-day aspects into a single personification, and the uninitiated who read of him take him as an individual and are very often at a loss to fit the various adventures and the various facets of character which he may show into some semblance of continuity. But as the story of the Western Tradition unfolds itself, perhaps it will be more simple to see the development of the personifications and to appreciate how the story unrolls itself, gathering new material and new presentation of the old.

In the interests of the next great dispensation, that of the Christian Faith, the story of Arthur has been so interwoven with the Christian aspects and the legends of the saints and of the Grail that it is not always easy to remember that the Arthurian cycle comes to us from the beginnings of time. Long, long before the Church of Christ was instituted, long, long before the coming of the Christ Himself, the great Ones of the Mysteries lived and worked and taught and had their being in these islands under their generic names of Merlin, Morgan and Arthur.

There was a Grail and a Spear long before the coming of the Christ and it is with these earlier days that this book will be chiefly concerned; the Christian symbolism of the Arthurian cycle has been so fully dealt with by others that it would be both impertinent and unnecessary to attempt to develop it further. It is there for those who would learn more of it but it is as well to remember that this symbolism is based on something infinitely older – preceding Christianity by almost untold ages. For what indeed are the Christian Grail and the Christian Spear if they are not the cup and the wand of the magician translated into a later symbolism? In the older Arthurian Cycles and in the legends of the Grail we have the Mystery Tradition of our race.

The oldest mysteries were based on intuition and clairvoyance. This was the first Wisdom; the Wisdom of the All-Seeing Eye, which is the power that functions through that third centre of vision lying between the optics and, roughly speaking, in the centre of the forehead or the bridge of the nose. This is the Eye of Vision and in those early days it was a real and living organ. Nowadays books are written to try and help people to re-develop it again under the more usual name of the Third Eye; in the periods intervening man has come further down into matter and the power of the Eye, for centuries dormant save in the most exceptional cases, is now to be revived on the higher arc of ascension. In the early days men had not developed sufficiently for the evolution of the powers of reason; they were instinctive, psychically aware of their surroundings, intuitive to an extremely high degree and working by their knowledge of the inner planes. In the course of evolution it was necessary that they should lose this power, pass through the Age of Instinct to the Age of Reason and gradually come round full circle to the re-awakening of the higher centres. It is to this period of re-awakening that we are now slowly progressing.

The story of the change is hidden in the Mysteries of our early days. In the next chapter, dealing with the Pantheons of our ancestors, some light will be shed on the development through the centuries. It must be remembered that in all cases where a race is 'conquered' by another race, either in legend or in half-history, the change usually indicates an alteration in the aspects of the ruling pantheon and a period of further development on the lines of evolution. There is a legend that the Gods of the Shining Land of Death once ruled in Ireland. The Land of Death indicates some land across the water, for to the early people all those across the sea were of another category. The Shining Land of Death is a comprehensible name for Atlantis, where the great Temple of Poseidon was faced with Orichalcum, which has the shining look of white gold in the sunlight and where Death came with such terrifying suddenness.

When the rule of the early gods came to its appointed end, the men from the Land of Death came, conquered and drove them from their temples. Of their followers it is said that half of them went to the West and the other half to the caves. It must be remembered that the new light, the new period of evolution, wherever it may come from geographically is referred to as coming from the East, the land of the rising sun, as at a later period the light of the Star was to be seen 'in the East', though the Wise Men would have travelled west to Bethlehem. From time immemorial the dying era has faded into the west with the dying sun. East and West are symbolic of birth and death rather than of geographical points and should not be taken literally.

The caves are always symbolic of the receptacles of the inner wisdom, that which is hidden. And when half the Gods went to the west and the other half to the caves, we are but reading that the practice of the older mysteries died out as the newer ones came in, but that the hidden wisdom, the true knowledge, persisted, as it must always do, to carry the stream of light through the countless cycles. Now the development of a more material age and the age of reason had to come into being for the evolution of the soul of man, and for a time the wisdom had to be communicated secretly and only to those who could understand it. There is always a period of darkness at the beginning of every new cycle; a period which corresponds in nature to the darkness of the womb, whether it be of man, of animal or of vegetable; then come the birth pains and the new life struggles into existence, blind and feeble at first but still carrying within it the germ of that wisdom which it has learnt, however imperfectly, during the silence and darkness of the period of gestation. The wisdom is always learnt in the silence and in the darkness; it is manifested in the light of day and the bustle of the world, but it cannot be learnt until the being is stilled.

From the beginning of time Britain was thought of as a holy isle. Doubtless the great priests of Atlantis who could foresee the future and knew what must befall their own land and their own period of evolution had already visioned it as the cradle of the next generation of the wise men, the receptacle of the Hidden Wisdom.

And so, rising out of the sea in the west, it stood with Ireland as the symbol of the home of the mysteries before ever they were brought over to be practised and developed among its woods and hills.

Before ever it was inhabited, it was called Merdin, the dweller in the sea – the land abiding in the west like a star. It was also called in the early days Clas Myrddin, or the Enclosure of Merlin, and later on it was called the Honey Isle of Beli – the sweet island, for honey is the food of the gods – rising from the sea, known in old Welsh literature as Beli's Drink, while the waves are called Beli's cattle. In the West of England to-day may still be found Bell Knowe or Beli's Hill, which was originally water-surrounded when the Brue and other Somerset rivers spread over their banks and formed the great marshes of the Rhineland.

Astrologically, Merlin is Mercury, the evening star, who changes place with his twin sister, Gweddyd, who is Venus. These are the interchangeable planets, symbols of the masculine and feminine, the two pillars which play and interplay with their power between positive and negative, one of which is never complete without the other, the pair of opposites which being equated gives balance. And so Merlin is also Mercury, or Thoth or Hermes, the teacher of Divine Wisdom, from whom comes the knowledge of the Word, while his sister is his counterpart, the awakening life or soul of the mysteries, who gives the form to his teaching, who is the recipient of his knowledge and who with him creates the perfect pair for the propagation of the perfect third. For the twins, Mercury and Venus, Merlin and Morgan, suggest the moment between sleeping and waking, the time when souls are best prepared to receive impressions of the shining lands beyond our human knowledge.

A bard of the sixth century has written -

> Knowest thou what thou art
> In the hour of sleep –
> A mere body – a mere soul –
> Or a secret retreat of the light?

and here is postulated that age-old riddle – where does the spirit go when the body lies in slumber? Many theories, many doctrines have been put forward; many wise men can recall their 'dreams' and their 'visions' and none would deny them. But the language of symbol is hard to understand and it is unproven where the spirit travels while the body sleeps. In *The Flaming Door* Eleanor C. Merry writes:

> The original Hibernian Mysteries were a way to the remembrance of Atlantis, to the vision of the beginning of Man, even long before Atlantis, and in the Beginnings the vision of the great Enigma of the future, the Apocalypse.

The original working of the Mysteries looked first backwards and then forwards, and upon their basic teaching we may find the traditions and mysteries of our Western Schools. In those early days the two great principles were those of Knowledge and of Beauty, sometimes called Science and Art, symbolized by two great figures, one male and one female. These were the two fundamental principles of those early days – Wisdom and Beauty – and the experience of the initiate in these first mysteries was to become conscious of the third great principle – the warmth and strength of Love, later exemplified to the world in the coming of the Christ.

The old priests of the Hibernian Mysteries knew that He would come. They initiated their neophytes in the path of Love, but though they demanded faith of their followers they themselves knew that it was only a question of time. They could see clairvoyantly that One was on His way who would bring this third great principle among men in its supreme earthly form and would bring it into actual materialization that it might be seen and in some small way understood by those who were to be born again in the uncounted generations of the future and whose work in this material world would be to live that Love united with the Wisdom and Beauty of the first mysteries, so that in due course the Perfect Man might be evolved, standing with the unyielding balance of the perfectly aligned.

The priests even before His coming spoke of Him as a living Being not yet in material manifestation; they saw Him clairvoyantly and spoke of Him as one who would come to give the gift that comes only of the Spirit – Strength in the Heart. So deeply were they versed in their work as seers, so developed their clairvoyant perceptions, that it was the Priests of the Hibernian Temples and of no others who were able to report the happenings of the

Crucifixion in all its details at the very hour when it was being enacted.

The Crucifixion became indelibly confused with the stories of the ancient gods. Fiona MacLeod relates how an old woman of Appin, Jessie Stewart, told him that when Christ was crucified He came back to earth as Oisin of the Songs, the young God of Love and Life. A ferryman on Loch Etive near the Falls of Lora told how on the day that Christ was crucified Oisin slew his own son and knew madness, crying out that he was but a shadow and his son was but a shadow, and that what he had done was in itself but a shadow of what was being done in that hour 'to the black sorrow of time and the universe'. On that day, too, Concobar MacNessa, High King of Ulster, rose suddenly from his seat and fled into the woods. There he was found, hewing down the branches of trees and crying that he slew the multitudes of those who at that very moment were doing to death the innocent son of a king.

These then were the seeds, the nursery garden of our Western Mystery Tradition; on these precepts was it founded and on them has it grown. No person seriously considering it could refuse to admit the security of its foundation and the line of power through which it has been handed down. The power may have become tenuous and the line waver but the true succession of the knowledge has never been lost.

Let us then trace the story of our heritage further until it is linked with names that are at least familiar to us, though not perhaps in the setting in which we are most accustomed to find them.

Chapter 2

The Ancient Gods

To disentangle the pantheons of the ancient Western tradition is not an easy business. It needs a clear head and above all the awareness that the gods, by whatever name they may be called, are but the personifications of the powers that lie behind them. So whereas we may have generations of Merlins and Morgans, carrying on the cognomens and in themselves functioning ever upon the same lines, so in the pantheons the situation is reversed and we have the same gods appearing under continually varying names. For as each phase in the development of the mysteries took place, so, generally speaking, did the outward name of the god-aspect change.

According to one who devoted many years to the study of the Western tradition, the three essential features of the ancient religions were Myth, Magic and Mystery. Myth, he maintains, means a series of conventional symbols used as an aide to memorizing. Magic is the art of causing change to take place in consciousness in accordance with will. Mystery is the secret teaching of the initiate; it is that which is not given out.

This dictum that myth means a series of symbols is of the greatest importance when we are considering the gods of our first ancestors. This accounts for the change of names in the gods whose symbols are the same but who are called by different appellations.

The information generally in regard to these very early years is gathered from certain old manuscript sources. Naturally these vary in date and none of them are contemporary with the events, for at that time, quite apart from the facilities for permanent record making, all tradition was oral and it would have been considered highly improper to attempt to set it down in any other way.

But the chief sources for the Irish tradition are to be found in the *Book of the Dun Cow*, composed or collected by one Maelmuiri in 1100 or thereabouts; the *Book of Leinster*, by Finn mac Gorman, Bishop of Kildare, which dates from the early part of the twelfth century; and two rather later volumes, the *Book of Ballymote* and the *Yellow Book of Lecan*, of the end of the fourteenth century, followed during the next hundred years by the *Book of Lecan* and the *Book of Lismore*.

As a comment on the age of the Irish legends, it is said that the exploits of Cuchullin had not only been turned into a saga but by the seventh century AD it was already forgotten as obsolete by the Bards. Indeed Senchan Torpeist, the chief bard of Ireland, received permission to raise Fergus, the contemporary of Cuchullin and a leading actor in the Raiding of the Cattle of Cooley, that from the grave he might recount once more the story lest it should be entirely forgotten.

The Scottish authorities are manuscripts chiefly preserved in the National Library of Scotland at Edinburgh; better known still to most students as the Advocates' Library. Generally speaking, they corroborate the Irish stories, add to the Cuchullin Saga and also contain stories of the Tuatha da Danaan, but they are themselves chiefly of the fifteenth and sixteenth centuries, though there are a few of the fourteenth.

Wales possesses the Four Ancient Books of Wales. From these the stories of the Mabinogion have been drawn, the poems of Taliesin and such other materials as were finally written down when the old tradition of oral handing-down died out. From these written scripts some of the mystery teaching which would otherwise be lost to us can be assessed and fitted into place. The Four Books are the *Black Book of Caermarthen* (the Book of the Seat or Chair of Math), which was written down in the reign of Henry II and attributes its poems to Myrddin – one of the bards bearing that generic name. The *Book of Aneurin* was compiled in the latter part of the twelfth century and the *Book of Taliesin* at the beginning of the fourteenth. These contain material attributed respectively to bards of these names. The Fourth Book is the *Red Book of Hergest*, now at Cambridge, and compiled in the fourteenth and fifteenth centuries. The work of this is believed to be that of Llywarch Hen. All these Bards are thought to have existed in the sixth century AD, which is apparently the Golden Age of our tradition in so far as the collection and perpetuation are concerned.

Before going into the question of nomenclature and the succession of one to the other, it might be a good idea to try and put the mythological history of our islands into some sort of perspective – to get some idea of sequence, of timing and of development.

Mythology seems to cling more closely and with more detail to Ireland than to the rest of Britain individually. Away in the dawn of time the first inhabitants of Ireland were said to be the Fomors – primeval, hideous monstrosities who came out of the sea – whose name actually means 'under sea' folk. Here is myth in its true form, for the Fomors were no doubt the symbols evolved by the most primitive for those monsters of the deep which once crawled over the earth. They were known, too, as the Children of Domna or darkness; one of their great gods who has come down to us in legend to this day as the mighty Buirraineach had his shrine under a tumulus in the heart of Ireland, and his name, no doubt with reference to his appearance, means 'Cow-headed'.

As the world evolved, the men of earth fought the former denizens of the sea. Two strange races of whom little if anything is known, are said to have come to Ireland and fought the Fomors.

The first of these was the Race of Partholon, said to have come from the Summer Country, a misleading term, since in the early Keltic literature it frequently means from the Other World, which in itself also meant from beyond the waters, where the knowledge of the inhabitants of Britain had not penetrated. It can also imply godly descent and is part of the origin of the godly and royal ancestry of many of the heroes. The leader of this race is reputed to have come with a retinue of twenty-four young men and twenty-four young girls and to have landed in Ireland on Beltaine Day, the First of May, the day of the Lord of the Underworld. This small group not only increased in size itself but in some way actually is reputed to have increased the size of Ireland, being responsible for a number of loughs, hills and pasture land. They fought the Fomors and conquered them, and for the space of three hundred years there was peace in the land. Then a sudden and unexplained epidemic attacked the whole of the race of

Partholon, beginning on the First of May, and within seven days the entire company was dead.

This strange race was followed by another, the Race of Nemed of whom even less seems to be recorded in the old stories. These new settlers also fought the Fomors and beat them back in four battles, but the length of their peace was much less than three hundred years and then they, too, were wiped out by an epidemic.

These two little known races were followed by the people known as the Fir Bolgs. They, too, are said to have come from the Other World and were perhaps Iberian in origin. Tradition says that they came from Spain, which was one of the names used for Hades, the land beyond the dark waters. The Fir Bolgs organized the country in their fight with the Fomors and apparently forced them to give up the struggle for supremacy for the time being. Five parts of Ireland did the Fir Bolgs create – Ulster, North and South Munster, Leinster and Connaught – and at the centre of the country they placed the Hill of Uisnech, where the five provinces touched one another. So well did they establish themselves that they are credited with nine supreme kings, the last of whom was Eochaid, son of Erc the Proud.

In all the mythology of Ireland there is no chapter more fascinating or perhaps better known, at least in outline, than the story of the Tuatha da Danaan. They have lived through the centuries because they are the forebears, ancestors and even originals of the Fairy folk. It is they who became the Lordly Ones, dwelling in the hollow hills, the fairy hills called the sidhe, which gave their name to the race who dwelt within them.

The Tuatha da Danaan came from their four cities, one for each quarter of the earth, and each one of them yielding one of the four treasures of the people. From Finias in the South came the Fiery Spear of the Sun God, the emblem of life-giving force; from the West came the Cup of Healing, the water of life; from the East came the Sword of Light that should fight against darkness; and from the dark, mysterious North there came the Stone of Destiny, the Lia Fail, which tradition says rests now in the Coronation Chair. Four cities there were, Finias, Murias, Gorias and Falias, 'the four cities at the four ends of the green diamond that is the earth. That in the north was made of earth; east, air; south, fire; and west, water. In the middle of the green diamond that is the world is the Glen of Precious Stones. It is in the shape of a heart and glows like a ruby, though all stones and gems are there. It is there that the Sidhe go to refresh their deathless life.'

With them came the worship of the great Mother Goddess, the first of her kind, Danu, whose children they called themselves. Danu runs through the mythology of all our Western tradition, her name changes with the pantheons but she herself is ever the same, the great primeval mother of our race, whether she be called Danu or Ana or, as in Ephesus, Di-ana, whose statue was one of the Seven Wonders of the World and showed her as the mother of all living. Danu is akin to Rhea, mother of all the gods, and her husband is Bile, the god of the underworld, and their son Nuanda of the Silver Hand, whose names will come again with variation. For 'all the gods are one god' and though they may change their names and even split up their attributes in the various aspects with a different god-name for each, yet still they are themselves the same from the beginning of time. 'In the beginning God created the world' and from that moment all divinities must be aspects of the One God; a belief which is more clearly demonstrated when the day of the Keltic Pantheon is reached. But in these early days when all is shrouded in the mists of the eternal sea, the clouds that veil the Summer Lands and the dark land that lies beyond the waters, we can only catch a name here and there and glimpse a personification that can be identified but not pinned down to form, only gradually taking shape under a new name as the world slowly evolves out of the darkness of the void.

Of Dana, 'A.E.' has written:

So is Dana the basis of every material form from the imperishable body of the immortals to the transitory husk of the gnat. As this divinity emerges from its primordial state of ecstatic tenderness or joy in Lir, its divided rays, incarnate in form, enter upon a threefold life of spiritual love, of desire and the dark shadow of love; and these three states have for themselves three worlds into which they have transformed the primal nature of Dana: a World of Immortal Youth; a Mid-World where everything changes with desire; and which is called from its fluctuations the World of Waters; and, lastly, the Earth World where matter has assumed that solid form when it appears inanimate or dead.

In her aspect as the Goddess of War and Wrath, her Gwrach or virago aspect, according to the Kabbalistic Tree of Life, or her Kali aspect in the Eastern theology, Dana comes to us as that dreaded goddess of the Irish myths, the Morrigan or Morrigu. Her name means simply the Great Queen, the Mor Righ Anu, and terrible indeed are some of the descriptions of her in the Irish stories. She has survived to this day as the 'Awful Warning'.

Dagda, the father, the Zeus of this early pantheon, has also survived in story. His wife was Boann, who gave her name to the River Boyne. Near where the head of the Boyne now lies, was a sacred well, round which grew nine hazel trees. The ripe nuts from these trees contained all the secrets of wisdom and for that reason they were carefully guarded. When ripe they fell into the well, where dwelt the sacred salmon, who fed upon them and thereby became the symbol of wisdom in the West. Desirous of obtaining knowledge, Boann, like Eve, stretched out her hand to the forbidden fruit, but in this case it was the well which took charge. The waters rose in a great wave and rushed out like a torrent, sweeping Boann away and spreading over the countryside, so that the river called Boyne was formed.

The children of Dagda were Brigit, Mider, Angier, Ogmas and Badb the Red. Of them all, Brigit was the best known and loved and so much has she become a part of the story of the Western Mysteries that there is a chapter on her alone elsewhere in this book.

Mider was king of the Underworld and had his castle in Falga, which was the old name for the Isle of Man. For it must be remembered that at this remote date the other side of the Irish Sea was the Other World to those dwelling on either side of it; the Irish and the Welsh each considered the other to be in Hades. Mider figures in the Irish legends after the Tuatha da Danaan had been driven from the land and it is he who comes from the mists and the underworld to seek Etain, Eochaid's wife, in 'The Immortal Hour'.

Ogmas became the god of literature and it is supposedly to him that the Ogham alphabet is due. He married one of the numerous minor goddesses called Etain, in this case a daughter of Dianecht, the god of healing and medicine.

And behind them all was the strange, shadowy form of the greatest of all the gods – Lir, the soul of the sea. 'A.E.' says:

> In the beginning was the boundless Lir, an infinite depth, an invisible divinity, neither dark nor light, in whom were all things past and to be ... Of Lir but little may be affirmed, and nothing can be revealed ... an infinite being, neither spirit nor substance but rather the spiritual form of these, in which all the divine powers raised above themselves exist in a mystic union or trance. This is the night of the gods from which Manannan first awakened, the most spiritual divinity known to the ancient Gael, being the Gaelic equivalent to that Spirit which breathed on the face of the waters ... Manannan is still the Unuttered Word, and is in that state the Chaldaic Oracle of Proclus saith of the Divine Mind: 'it had not yet gone forth, but abode in the Paternal Depth, and in the Dytum of god-nourished silence'.

But the Golden Age of the Tuatha da Danaan did not last for very long. From over the dark waters came the Milesians, led by Mile, a demi-god, who came ostensibly to avenge the death of his father Bile. He brought with him, according to the Irish Book of Conquests, his wife Scota, daughter of the Pharaoh, who gave her name to Scotland, and also his chief Druid and Bard, Amergin of the Fair Knee, who was the first man ashore when the boat grounded on the shingle. He is the corresponding figure to that of the Welsh bard Taliesin, and his song on the Battle between the Milesians and the Tuatha da Danaan has much in common with the Song of the Battle of the Trees.

And so the Tuatha da Danaan were driven out from the fair land they loved. Some of them went to the land of Tir n'an Oige, the Land of the Ever Young, and the others stayed within the sidhe or fairy hills, which have doors leading down to Tir n'an Oige and yet give access to earth. And it is from these fairy hills that the remnants of the Tuatha da Danaan have taken their other name of People of the Sidhe or more simply the Sidhe.

The Land of Tir n'an Oige is very dear to the hearts of all who are steeped in the Western Mystery teaching. It is the place of repose; the resting place of our mother race; sometimes, looking down through clear water, it can be glimpsed faintly where a little stream runs silently beneath a bridge with a birch tree and an alder at either end. That is where the two worlds may touch at sunset, but it is not wise for the student or the tyro to venture out of his own element into that faery land; before he can travel safely in so foreign a country he must learn the way to return, or he will find himself drifting helplessly for ever in the twilight, neither admitted beyond the fairy portals nor able to return to take up his earth life. That is the land of Illusion, which the student of the mysteries must learn to recognize and pass through on his way to the true Moon country.

They say the Sidhe ride 'Hosting' and, fanciful though it may seem to some, there are those who in their working of the Western Mysteries have said they have seen that in Tir n'an Oige there also dwell the spirits of those well loved and individualized animals who have been developed into 'way-showers', the leaders of their genus, those who have attained nearer to individuality than the masses. For that there must be a slow but gradual individualization of the animal kingdom has been recognized by man, who sees also that beyond that goal lie the similar aspirations of the plants and the minerals, and it is a part of our duty and our privilege to help in the course of evolution by assisting the way-showers in their task. The mounts of the Sidhe are those horses which have been individualized by the love of their masters, and who now gallop through the air bearing the shining ones upon their backs. They have been seen and recognized – Marengo, Bellerophon, White Surrey, The Maltese Cat, and all horses and mares dear to their former owners upon this plane. And so we may believe that one day we shall meet not only the members of our own evolution but our younger brethren, to whom we owe care and thought and indeed instruction and guidance, and they and we will recognize one another in that great day of rejoicing when we pass through the land of Tir n'an Oige.

And from that lovely Land of Youth comes that Child of the Gods, dear to the hearts of all who work with the Western Mysteries, Angus Og, Angus MacGreigne, Angus the Ever Youthful, the Son of the Sun, the Young Horus of our house of the Gods. He may be called Spring or Love or Death, for the elemental gods have always the three aspects to their natures. He walks this earth as the Loving Child, the Eternal Youth, the

Spirit of the Hearts of those who never grow old. Legend says that he goes to and fro upon the world, weaving rainbows, at whose further end lie not the crocks of gold but the way to the golden country of Tir n'an Oige.

There is another name for it, too, the House of Hades or the House of the Shadows. For that is the land to which the Keltic heroes travelled when they voyaged in the glass boat of initiation which took them out of this plane and into the worlds that lie beyond. It is that inner world which lies behind the dark door of the Temple Sanctuary and where the Guardians are the Angels of the Gods of the Race; we have our right to admittance through that door, for we are of the old tradition and the old Blood. It is a land to which a child may go more easily than an adult for the door opens only to the simple and the humble ... 'except ye become as little children'. Philosophers and scientists have longed to find the way but have not possessed the key to the door.

Each man must find his own key and none other will admit him. One such key is hinted at by Plato when he wrote 'Beloved Pan, and all ye other Gods who haunt this place, give me beauty in the inward soul; and may the outward and the inward man be as one.' And the Persian Hafiz epitomized the purpose of the quest in his saying, 'The objects of all religions are alike. All men seek their beloved and all the world is love's dwelling'.

Manannan son of Lir is, it might be said, the bridge, the transition between the pantheon of Ireland and that of Scotland and Wales. It is said the Manannan was the special guardian of the Irish travellers when they went to foreign parts and that this guardianship continued until the days of Columba.

Now it so happened that Columba broke his golden chalice and sent his servant with it to the goldsmith to have it mended. And while the servant was upon the road it so chanced that he met with Manannan, who asked him what he was about. On being shown the chalice, the god breathed upon it and the two pieces were joined by a miracle. He gave it back to the astonished servant saying to him, 'Tell him to whom this belongs that Manannan son of Lir who mended this desires to know if he will ever gain Paradise.' Unfortunately St Columba was more shocked at the power which had mended his chalice than moved at the rather touching wording of the message, and he exclaimed 'There can be no forgiveness for a man who does works such as these.' Not unnaturally Manannan took offence at this cruelty and remarked with some bitterness 'For years I have helped the Catholics of Ireland but I'll do it no more, and go to the grey waves of the Highlands.' And so he was seen no longer in Ireland but established himself in a palace called Emain Abhlach or Emain of the Apple Trees, situated on the Isle of Arran in the Firth of Clyde. There he kept his three swords, the Avenger or Retaliator, Great Fury and Little Fury, and his two magical spears, Yellow Shaft and Red Javelin.

In an article published in *The Occult Review* of 1902 and titled 'Sea Magic and Running Water', Fiona Macleod tells how an old man of eighty in the Hebrides would often be visited in his *shieling* by a tall beautiful stranger with a crest on his head 'like white canna blowing in the wind but with a blueness in it' and 'a bright cold curling flame under the soles of his feet'. He would talk to Murdo MacIan and tell him many things, even to the foretelling of the day of his dying. He wore a white cloak that hid his hands but once he moved to touch the shepherd and it could be seen that his flesh was like water with seaweed floating among the bones. Then the shepherd knew that his visitor was none other than Manannan, the great god.

The gods of Britain go hand in hand with the gods of Ireland and in many cases there is only a slight change of name. They are born of the same parentage, and until we come from the earliest days to the establishment of the great Druid worship and its pantheon there is little but a change of name to remember.

The British gods were divided into two great families, the Children of Don or the Children of Nudd, and the Children of Llyr. Don is Dana, the great earth mother, and Llyr is of course Lir, the ruler of the great waters. The Children of Don are listed as Gwydion, Gilvaethy, Amatheon, Govannon and Arianrhod, who had twin sons, Dylan and Llew. With most of these it is not necessary to concern oneself too much, but Gwydion should be borne in mind. He is not only the god of poetry and divination but also the philosopher and culture bringer, and Sir John Rhys thinks that he should be considered as the forerunner of Arthur. For according to this theory, Arthur and his Knights are the development of the ancient gods of Britain.

Not unnaturally, the Children of Don provide names for many of the constellations of the Western Hemisphere. That which we know as Casseopeia's Chair is Llyr Don, the Court of Don. The Northern Crown is Arianrhod, whose personal symbol is also the rainbow, while the Milky Way is the Castle of Gwydion. Later on Arthur takes his place as the Great Bear and the Lyre is his harp.

Nudd or Lludd is the son of Don and her husband Beli, who is as much a king of the underworld as his Irish counterpart Bile. Nudd is the Zeus of the pantheon in Britain and is also called Llaw Ereint or Silver-Handed, which immediately equates him with Nuanda. He fathered Gwynn ap Nudd, who became the King of the Fairies, which is to say lord of the underworld. He is the conductor of the dead and, in another aspect, leads the Hounds of Hell on their nightly riding. These are called the Yeth Hounds of Somerset, and Glastonbury Tor has been considered one of the chief haunts of Gwynn. Somerset is of course only a variation of the Summer Land or the Land beyond Death, and the Vale of Taunton was in old days known as Paradise.

Llyr, father of Manawyddan, was lord of the sea, and Lir and Manannan were its lords in the Irish story. Llyr's other two children were Bran and Branwen, both of whom are connected with the underworld.

The real king of the Welsh underworld was Pwyll, the Crane, who ruled it with his wife Rhiannon and his son Pryderi. In many of the early stories he is represented as being hostile to the children of Don but friendly to those of Llyr. In the course of time Pwyll disappears from the pantheon and Rhiannon becomes the wife of Manawyddan, God of Elysium, and according to one of the Taliesin poems, Hades is jointly ruled for a time by Manawyddan and Pryderi, who kept the famous cauldron which runs through all the earliest Western mysteries; that cauldron which in one guise or another is the chalice of the West, the source of inexhaustible sustenance.

Llew is the Apollo of the Keltic reading and Diodorus refers to the 'magnificent Temple of Apollo', which is 'in the centre of Britain' and is possibly Stonehenge. Sir John Rhys is disposed to credit Stonehenge to the worship of Merlin, as Zeus, and Geoffrey of

Monmouth says that Merlin erected stones. But it seems reasonable to think that in those very early days there might well be some confusion or even fusion between the sky god and the sun god.

These are the early gods of the Britons as given in the collection of stories known as the *Mabinogion*. These are the first of the myths as we know them and from them the others have developed. This early group had its day and passed into another later group, known as the 'Taliesin'.

It is at this point that we can begin, perhaps, to assess a little more clearly the outlines of our Mystery Teachings. For now there is a little more firmness in the outlines; the myths in their present form continue to within a period that is at least comprehended by ourselves, though we may not know much about it. They are the same gods but they have forms and names that have a ring of familiarity about them.

Here is Keridwen with her cauldron, which is the subject of much discussion and so much speculation; the cauldron with its pearl embossed rim which would not cook the food of a coward nor of one that was not true at heart. In *The Ancient Secret*, Lady Flavia Anderson has given us a work of the greatest value, for she has collected and assessed all versions of the Grail story and has also given in much detail and with much documentation the origin of the Grail and what it really was. Such an evaluation is not a part of this book's purpose, but it should be remembered that the Cauldron is the sacred vessel of our Mystery Tradition, that it is the source of revelation before the coming of the Christian dispensation and that the Grail of the Christ teaching is but the natural development of the story of the Cauldron.

According to the old myth, Keridwen had a son of extreme ugliness called Avagddhu or Blackwings. Wishing to compensate him for his hideous aspect she determined to give him all wisdom. Cynddeleu the Bard sings 'How mysterious were the ways of the songs of Keridwen; how necessary to understand them in their true sense.' And in the *Book of Taliesin* we find 'Then Keridwen determined, agreeably to the mystery of the books of Pheryllt, to prepare for her son a cauldron of the water of inspiration and knowledge ... In the meantime Keridwen with due attention to the book of astronomy and to the hours of the planets, employed herself daily in collecting plants of every species which preserved any rare virtues.'

Having collected her materials, Keridwen set them to boil within her cauldron and instructed her servant, Gwyion, to watch the brew. She stirred it and as she did so Three Drops of Essence fell from the spoon and were caught by Gwyion upon his finger, which he immediately put to his mouth. By this means he and not Avagddhu became the possessor of all knowledge. It is a parallel to the story of Finn, the Irish god-hero, who touched one of the salmon of the Boyne and then put his finger in his mouth and found that the scale of the salmon having adhered to his own skin he had become the repository of wisdom.

Keridwen turned into a fury at the failure of her plan and chased Gwyion with the intent to kill him. Gwyion transformed himself into various forms in the hope of eluding her but to no purpose as she immediately took the shape of a new enemy. When he became a hare, she was a dog to worry him; when he turned into a fish, she was the otter and when he became a grain of wheat, she at once turned into a hen and swallowed him.

The hidden truths being what they are, it is only natural to learn that Keridwen subsequently gave birth to Gwyion who became her son. His name was changed to Taliesin the Wonder Child when he was abandoned by his mother, who cast him into the river whence he was drawn up as is the case with such other great ones as Moses and Jesus. Taliesin then takes his place in the Keltic pantheon as the Sun God, known in another aspect as Hu the Mighty, the God of Light.

Keridwen is known to us also, and perhaps more familiarly, as Cordelia, a corruption of her own earlier name Creiddylad, which means 'Daughter of the Sea', while her own daughter is the maiden Creirwy, who is Kore, and Persephone, the young spring.

The Tree of Life, as it is known to the Qabbalists, is the yardstick by which all the pantheons may be measured, since it cannot err. If they do not fit it, there is a slip somewhere in the aspects given to the gods. It can be tested throughout the world – Egypt, the East, Greece and Rome – all can be proved by its ruling. What is the Tree of Life? Briefly, it is the series of Emanations into manifestation of the Great Unmanifest, the God behind the Gods, descending into matter by a series of progressions and preparing eventually to reascend on the reverse journey. The lowest of these stages is that of the material world in which we are now living.

Only the simplest and briefest explanation can be given here; for those who are not familiar with the system, there are books devoted entirely to the subject, the best of which is probably *The Mystical Qabalah* by Dion Fortune.

The Tree of Life consists of Ten Sephiroth, as they are called, the first nine arranged in a series of three triangles and the last one dependent. Each Sephira leads from its predecessor to its successor so that there is no break in the continuity; each is, in fact, an overflowing of the previous one, as the power comes into manifestation. Each in turn manifests a different aspect of the Eternal Godhead from which they have all sprung.

The first of these Sephiroth is the Everlasting God, Light Eternal, the Crown, such are some of the names given to this Unknown Being; in the Hebrew it is *Kether*; in all the pantheons it is always the prime source of illumination and manifestation. The Kelts called him Kelu, the Source of All Life and called themselves Kelts because they were the Children of Kelu and therefore Sons of God. From this first Sephira a line can be drawn at an angle and downwards to the right where the second stage is placed. This is symbolized by the Zodiac and in the Keltic Pantheon by the Wheel or Rhod, the Wheel of Life. Draw a line to the left from this Wheel and make a triangle with a line from the left of the first Sephira; this is the place of the Mother of all Living. Here you will find the great Mothers in their primordial being. Keridwen, Hera, the first great Isis; they all correspond to the Wheel of Life, the Father God, Zeus on the opposite side. Each of these two spills over as it were into a point below it, that on the feminine side being in the Keltic Gwrach, the virago, and in the other pantheons the war goddesses. Here is Kali, the destroyer, for woman is the destroyer that man may be born again. Woman is death in life and life in death; her first symbol is water, the Dark Sea, the Bitter Water of Marah. Below Rhod, the Wheel, is Ked, the Protector, the God of Justice, Mars in his finer aspect, the righter of wrong, the King and father of the people. And by a line drawn inwards and downwards from each of these two the next Sephira is reached, lying in a direct line beneath the first great Manifestation. This is the place of the Sun Gods, of the Healers of Men, of the Sacrificed Gods; it is known as the Heart Centre and in the Hebrew *Tiphareth*. Here are Baldur and Attis and Jesus the Christ and Hu-Taliesin.

Let this Sun Centre be the apex of your next triangle which duplicates on the lower plane the first great triangle and on the Sephira on the right hand side below Ked, place one of the twins, Venus, while Mercury rests below Gwrach. These are the brother and sister gods, positive and negative to each other. On Venus, or *Netzach* goes the love goddess Aphrodite, Venus herself and Gwen, the nature goddess of the Kelts; for *Netzach* is the love of nature, the young spring green, the doves, the violets and the singing of the mating birds. And the opposite to this joyous fecundity is the fecundity of the mind, the complementary qualities. Here then stand Mercury and Thoth and Merlin and Gwyion, son of Keridwen when he had come from knowledge to kingship. And from these two emanates another Sephira again on that centre line below Taliesin, the Sephira of the Moon and of the astral world, where we place Arianrhod, the Rainbow, the reflector of the light. Then, pendant to this hangs otherwise alone the Earth, the material world in which we have to live and move but need not and should not have our spiritual being. That can rise through the mysteries of the Sephiroth until it should, even while we are in the world, be possible for it to unite itself with the Heart of the World in the Sun Centre.

This is the barest outline of the system, but it will just suffice to indicate the method to those who know nothing of it, while to those who do, it will not be necessary to discuss it at all, since they will long ago have tested the proof of it for themselves. But it is important that it should be appreciated that the Western Mystery Tradition will stand up to the measuring rod of the Tree and that it is as clearly defined as any other, though since it has been allowed to drop into desuetude, the nomenclature may well be unfamiliar to those who have not studied it.

It is a curious thing that we have by means of classical education in the past absorbed into current conversation and have at least a bowing acquaintance with the gods and goddesses of both Greece and Rome; most of us are aware of at least the leading figures of the Indian and Egyptian pantheons, yet how many could speak with familiarity of our own mother goddess, of Gwen and Gwyion as easily as of Venus and Mercury? It is a sad truth that a prophet is without honour in his own household and we have too long neglected those who gave us the glorious heritage which is ours today.

As we have seen, the names change but the faces are the same. Gwydion has passed but Arthur has come.

Let us then see what part Arthur played in the days before he was turned into the Champion of Christendom.

Chapter 3

Arthur

Arthur is the king of myth, of legend and of history who under this name has survived throughout the ages and is still a name known to every child. King Arthur and his Knights are the subject of countless books; the adventures of his band of brothers have been analysed, dissected and broken down into an elaborate series of symbols covering the whole journey of the soul of man and his eternal quest for the Highest. With this Arthur we do not deal in this book; ours is the Arthur behind the Christian mysteries, the Arthur who was the Sun-God and the King of the older dispensation and as such one of the guardians of our land.

His story is in effect the re-telling of the story of Math son of Mathonwy in the *Mabinogion*. Another story says that he is to be identified with Airem of the old Irish myth. There are two stories of Airem; Professor Rhys says that Arthur and Airem come from a common root and that Airem and Emer were the twin sons of Mil (or Golam) and are the Keltic correspondence of Romulus and Remus. Emer is supposed to have been the ancestor of these dwellers in Ireland who were not Kelts and to have been in due time slain by Airem, the Keltic chief. Airem wedded Etain, the daughter of the fairy king Etar, and she was carried off by Mider King of the Underworld as Guinevere was carried off by Modred. There is a further similarity here for both Etain and Guinevere were daughters of fairy kings and the root of each name means shadowy – they are the mystical feminine counterpart for whom the King is ever seeking; they are the Moons to his Sun.

Airem or Arthur is the new young Sun, the god in his heyday, where Aran is the name of the old one, who has given his name to Arran. The long night of 20 December, which in the old working was 25 December, was remembered in the Druid proverb Hir yw'r nos – aros Aran; Long is the night, waiting for Aran.

Arthur then stands for the Sun, the giver of life, the ruler of the world. He is the gardener who makes the crops to swell. Another version of his name is Artor which means Workman. He is always active; he is the third person of the Trinity which is composed of himself, Merlin the magician and Morgan the priestess. In Druid mythology he is the King, corresponding to Jupiter, who Mr Robert Graves points out is really Iu-pater, the Sun Father, the Giver of Life. His sign in the Zodiac is that of Aries the Ram, the owner of the Golden Fleece, the *Summum bonum* of his evolutionary period.

Like every other God-hero, Arthur had a mysterious birth. As Arthur, it is said that he was the offspring of a union between Uther Pendragon and Ygrain, Queen of Cornwall. Now as will be shown later, the Dragon was the sacred beast of the Druid mythology so that this birth is as symbolic as that of Jesus the Christ in a later dispensation. It is the union of Strength, as typified by the Great Dragon with the Beauty of Queen Ygrain. And as soon as the child was born, Merlin took him from the arms of his mother and carried him away to bring him up in the knowledge of the Mysteries, which is but an earlier substitution for the Journey into Egypt of a later date.

The mysterious begetting of the Wonder Child and his subsequent disappearance into fairyland, or what other name may be given to it, is common to all branches of the Keltic mythology as it is to the mythology of other lands. Arthur and Osiris have a common source; the Gardener of the West is fundamentally the same as the Fertility God of the Nile; Amenti is but Annwn, the dark country of the Keltic mysteries.

There is a strong resemblance between the Arthurian cycle and the story of Arjuna in the *Mahabrarata*, the repository of the Eastern Mysteries. With certain obvious changes which emerge in the natural differences between East and West, the student of either story will recognize the one he has first known in the variation he reads as second choice, regardless of which he takes first. In both histories the twin serpents are met with – the great dragons of the Pendragonship, which Arthur as a child was found playing with in his cradle. The sign of the serpent is never very far from

any Arthurian Seat; indeed one may be said to mark the presence
of the other. With an Arthurian legend in the locality you may look
for traces of serpent or dragon worship. The serpentine dance of
the white-robed priests is as familiar in the West as it is in the
East. The Serpent of Wisdom is one of those symbols which
permeate all mystery teachings and lead us to the acceptance of
their common origin and their ultimate universal goal.

What connection can be traced between the serpent worship
which is outlined in the *Mahabrarata* and that of the Keltic
teaching? When could they have met? Could the Indian serpent
myth be due to a Keltic original? There is a possibility of this in the
third century BC when Asoka, grandson of the heroic Chandra
Gupta, whom the Greeks call Sandracottus, became a convert to
Buddhism. At that time the Buddhist missionaries taught their
faith through Asia Minor and Syria and it is possible that they returned
to the East carrying with them such tales of spiritual value as they
might find in their wanderings.

In an article published a considerable time ago in the transactions
of the *Société des Antiquaires de France*, M. de Conquebert-
Montbret argues that the Asiatic missionaries who penetrated to
Western Europe reached as far west as Ireland and Scotland. He
asks if the ancient Gaelic deity named Budd or Budwas be not the
origin of Buddha. It is a fact that in the Hebrides spirits are
sometimes called Boduchas or Buddachs and the same word used
to be applied to the heads of families – i.e. Master.

On the other hand, it seems to be probably more likely that in
the great migration to the West of which more will be written in
the chapter on 'History', some of the Cimmerrii went East and
South. It has been pointed out that the intonations of the Cingalese
are very similar to those of the Welsh to-day and that it was quite
a surprise for a Western visitor to Ceylon to recognize the familiar
lilt of the Kelt. When we remember also that an island or a country
isolated by natural defences preserves its ancient customs and
languages much later than those lands where traffic with other
countries is common, then there is a good deal to be said for this
possibility.

Welsh tradition credits Arthur with three wives, each one of
them named Guinevere – and this is as it should be, for each of

them is an aspect of the triple goddess, who occurs again and again in the Western Mystery Tradition.

And what of the great fight for Arthur's life – the keeping of Guinevere? We are accustomed to thinking of Guinevere and Lancelot but that is a modern story foisted on to the old myth that the knight who abducted the Queen was none other than Modred or Medraut, the King's own cousin – or even the King's own other self. For if we go back to the earliest time of Airem we find Mider the King of the Underworld stealing the Queen from the sun, and we are standing once again on the threshold of that eternal combat of the Light and the Darkness for the Spring time. It is the King of Hades abducting the maid from Enna's fields; it is the triumph of the dying year. This, surely, is the story behind the story of Arthur and Guinevere and Modred.

With it goes that other great story which has been handed down through the centuries and personalized and vulgarized until it has become cheaply known as the Eternal Triangle. The story of the stolen bride is again the story of the two men at war for the woman; the man who does not understand the value of the soul, and who sees spiritual beauty snatched from him. Is it not in one sense a parallel to the parable of the man who buried his talent in a napkin?

The story of Diarmaid and Grania is the foundation story for all the myths and legends of its kind, including the story of Tristram and Iseult. And the tragedy lies not in the hopeless love of the man for the woman, a love which inevitably brings him to mortal death and disaster since he is engaged not in worldly success but in the acquiring of heavenly knowledge, but in the gradual and determined materialization of a world which is now so vulgarized as to take the story of the Heavenly Quest and turn it into the lowest form of so-called 'love'.

It is not possible to touch upon the story of even the pre-Christian Arthur and omit the Quest for the Holy Grail, for that Quest is the age-old Quest of man for union with the highest and precedes the Christian story by thousands of years. The Grail has been the Cauldron of Keridwen, the Cup of the Last Supper and many other things. Whatever material shape it may have taken, surely it is spiritually the union of man with the highest? Paradoxically can we not say that each man is himself his own Grail? Into him is poured the Life of God.

There is an old idea that the Grail was originally a Buddhist conception – a Buddhist relic which the Nestorians took over and brought to Persia where it was commingled with the teachings of the Manichees and became in the Middle Ages the Holy Grail. Another legend says that in that Cup the Mother of Jesus caught the blood that dripped from the wounds upon the Cross; it had to be hidden centuries later when the Moslems overran the Holy Land and then it was smuggled to Gaul. They say it shone 'like the moon of God' and brought fair winds in its train. Yet others say that it is the Gold Cup from the Temple of Ninunfa in the hidden lands of Asia and that it was a loving cup of the great Queen, filled with the blood of a beautiful slave and given to a lover to drink with musk and porphry as part of a Fertility Rite.

It was the Cup which was smuggled into Gaul which became the Holy Cup of Montsegur, the stronghold of the Albigenses. It was guarded by the Albigenses, also known as the Cathari or 'perfected ones'. When the orthodox Church rose up in its might against this stronghold of purity in Provence – a part of France that had always been to some extent isolated, where St Joseph of Arimathea was said to have landed and where his name was held in veneration – the man sent against the 'heretics' was the most bloodthirsty of his times – Simon de Montfort, the fanatic whose son later died at Evesham. On the 1st of March, 1244 the castle of Montsegur was betrayed by those whose faith was not strong enough to endure to the end. All those who had taken refuge therein were burnt in the meadow below, called ever after Champ des Cremats, but on the last night of February four courageous champions took the sacred Cup to safety and hid it in a place known only to themselves.

It is an interesting piece of traditional history, for the leader of the Albigenses at that time, the prime mover for the safety of the Grail, was a woman – Esclairmonde de Foix. Her story is one of the noble adventures of the period. It is said that when word was brought to her that the Cup was safely hidden her soul took flight and was carried to heaven in the form of a dove.

All one can really say is that the Grail is always the Cup of Life, and when man turns from that Life to the life of the material plane the Grail is taken from his sight and hidden by the Grail King, who is also known as the Rich Fisher, and whose symbol in Egypt is the Ibis, the sign of Thoth. He is the great Initiator, not the Initiated. He is of the line of the Lame Kings, from Pwyll, King of the Underworld to Amfortas in his Castle, for the Ibis is the same as the Crane in one respect, each stands on one leg with the other lifted, giving the appearance of lameness. The lameness or uneven gait was an early step towards a man's initiation into the mysteries, an initiation that took place by water – as that first initiation into the Church is still by water.

Arthur is the Keltic Messiah. That being so, he never dies but only sleeps until the time of his coming again is due.

He lives and dies therefore in many parts of his kingdom. Even the place of his final battle may be disputed. For many years, under the auspices of Malory and Tennyson, both of whom based their stories on the histories of Geoffrey of Monmouth and of Nennius, it was assumed that Arthur died but once and in the West of England and that Camelun where the final battle was fought was indeed Camelford. But there may be – and indeed there should be – as many Cameluns as there are Avalons. There is a suggestion that the last stand was made by the Camelan stream where it wanders down to Dolgelly through the arid waste of the Crawcwellt. The Welsh Triads say that Arthur and Modred fought at Camelan. They also say that they met in Nanhwynian (which is now Nant-y-Gwyant) three days before the battle, which would destroy any chance of the fighting having taken place at Camelford. And what could be a more likely spot than this wide valley, where the body of Arthur was finally carried down the estuary of the Mawddach and out to sea to a mystical Avalon? There is an Avalon in Caermarthenshire, as there is an Avalon at Glastonbury. There must surely be many Arthurs, many Camelans, and many Avalons where the mystic barge has rested since that last dreadful day when the glory of the cycle was broken.

In the dark barge lies the body of the dead King, across the knees of the three weeping Queens – the triple goddess of the great mysteries. Three Guineveres – Morgan le Fay, Nimue, the Lady of the Lake and Guinevere, the Queen – who knows? There were three women who stood by the Cross at Golgotha. When the King dies there are always three women by his side – the young woman, the wife and the mother; the Goddess attends the burial.

And so the barge takes Arthur down to Avalon, the Isle of Apples, where he rests neither dead nor alive but sleeping till the land shall have need of him again. Down in Glastonbury, which is Avalon in the West of England, the shallow mist which rises above the land with the Hunter's Moon and blots out all for a foot or two is still known as the Lake of Wonder, and there are those who even in this century have seen the black barge drift by with the three weeping Queens and the body of the dead King laid across their knees.

The death of Arthur is the death of a cycle of evolution; it is the end of a period which shall be renewed with the birth of the new Messiah who is indeed in one sense but a reincarnation of the old.

The resting places of Arthur and his Knights are many. The verses of the poem called 'The Graves of the Warriors', from the *Black Book of Caermarthen*, mentions the tombs of gods and demi-gods but ends 'Not wise the thought – a grave for Arthur', which Professor Sir John Rhys translates as 'Unknown is the grave of Arthur'.

In one legend the King sleeps in the Dinas Mountains with his knights around him. The Dinas Mountains are the mountains of Strength or Fortification and the king and his knights are considered to be the personified Hanvods or Emanations of the Sun. They have such names as light, heat, new souls, causes of vegetation and so forth. They lie within a mountain whose name can also be interpreted as Din (Dun), a fort and Aes, a Shield, amid heaps of gold and silver, each representing the active and passive forces. Craig y Dinas is in the Vale of Neath in South Wales.

Later English versions have placed the King's tomb in Winchester, while other stories place it at Pumsaint in Caermarthenshire, in Anglesey, Sewing Shields, Richmond, Yorks., and in Cadbury Camp in Somerset. To most of us who have been nurtured on the Western Mysteries our Avalon is Glastonbury.

Until recent years, shepherds in Wales regaled one another with stories of how one of their number had penetrated into the cave on Snowdon where Arthur lies sleeping amid his knights. The spiritual significance of Snowdon, the White Fort, is indicated

also by its ancient and poetic name of Y-Wyddea or the Presence.
The inscription on the tomb was reported to be 'Here Arthur lies,
King once and King to be', and of him Merlin prophesied that 'like
Dawn will he arise from his mysterious retreat'. Miss Jessie Weston
says that he is 'Lord of all fairy haunted spots', and it is said in
Scotland that the fairies sleep with him until he rise again. There
he rests beneath the Eildon Hills, not far from Edinburgh and just
without the holy earth of Melrose Abbey. This is his stronghold,
for he has his Seat also within the Capital – one that is mentioned
in the Gododin, the earliest British poem preserved in the Roman
alphabet, called by the Bards *Coelbren y Moneich*, or Alphabet
of the Monks.

There is an affinity, too, for Arthur with Wild Edric, the fairy
sleeper of Shropshire who rests under the Sliperstone Hills. He
too was a mighty rider and brought his bride from fairyland.

Fiona MacLeod tells the legend of Finn, the great Keltic hero,
who is but another form of Arthur, and of how a man stumbled
upon the mystery of that sleeping court. He lays the place in the
Western Isles that he knew so well, and it only shows how Arthur
sleeps in the hearts of men wherever they yet believe in the old
tradition.

He describes the discoverer: 'A man so pure that he could give
a woman love and yet let angels fan the flame in his heart, and so
innocent that his thoughts were white as a child's thoughts, and so
brave that none could withstand him, climbed once to the highest
mountain in the Isles where there is a great cave that no one has
ever entered.' When he reached the entrance to this cave he
found it guarded by a great white hound, asleep. He stepped across
its body but it did not stir. Then he entered the cave and passed
through a guard of four tall dark spirits with bowed heads and
folded arms. Their wings were all different but each was of one
of the mystic colours – white or red or green or black. They did
not raise their eyes as he went by. Beyond them in the heart of
the cave sat Finn and his Knights in a circle. Their long hair trailed
upon the ground; their eyebrows had grown down to mingle with
their beards and the beards themselves lay upon their feet, so that
to all outward seeming they had no bodies, for they were enveloped
each in his own hair. All that stood out from that mingling of hair

and beard and eyebrows were the hands like grey rock, clasped upon the hilts of the swords.

Behind them upon the wall hung an elk horn with its mouth-piece of gold; before them in the circle lay heaps of gold and silver and precious stones, treasure uncountable. Greatly daring, the man lifted the horn from the wall, set it to his lips and blew. Nothing stirred except the great white hound. It came slowly into the cave, pushed its way into the centre of the circle and sat down and began to eat of the treasure.

Daring still more, the man set the horn again to his lips and sent out a second blast. At the sound Finn and his Knights opened their great dead eyes, cold and lustreless, and stared at him. Then the man felt to the bones of him that he was standing by an open grave and he knew Fear – cold, impersonal Fear – for it seemed that the hand of a corpse had clutched his feet. Yet he must have been a brave man, or a foolhardy one, for in spite of his terror he blew the horn a third time and the echoes of its sound went round and round that cave till it reverberated with the loud notes. The effort of will was such that the sweat stood out on the man's forehead in great drops but still he waited.

And then he saw the Feinn move and lean upon their elbows, and as from very very far away but yet so loud that it echoed within the cave as the notes of the horn had echoed, Finn asked 'Is the end come?'. But the man could bear no more and he turned and fled, leaving that mighty host still leaning upon its elbows and waiting spellbound for the end. And so they wait still.

But the man himself heard behind him the sound of rushing wings and then a great gust of wind came and swung him off the mountain and as he fell he could hear the sound of demons as they dispersed into the heavens and he heard the baying of the white hound, and it was like the baying of no earthly dog ... and then the mountain had vanished and he was alone. He was found dead next day on the little island where he lived; there was no mark upon his body but there was a terrible fear in his eyes.

Another story tells how about the twelfth or thirteenth century a farmer of Mobberley had occasion to sell a beautiful white horse at the Macclesfield Fair. His road led along the heath not far from Alderley Edge. It was a lonely path and he was taken aback when he found himself confronted suddenly by a very tall monk, who barred his way with a staff of black wood. He informed the farmer that there was a finer fate awaiting the white horse than a sale at the Fair and ordered him to be at the same spot at sunset. Thinking little of it, the farmer rode on but it so happened that he could not get a bid for his beast and at sunset he found himself once more near Alderley Edge and face to face with the monk. By way of three local landmarks, Golden Stone, Stormy Point and Saddle Bole, the monk led him to a spot where neighing was heard beneath the ground. Striking the ground with his staff, the monk bade it open and a pair of iron gates came into view. Terrified beyond belief, both the farmer and the horse were compelled to obey the monk's command to pass through the gates. Within, in stalls on either side, were white horses similar to the farmer's own. Beside them were soldiers in old-fashioned armour, heaps of gold and silver in out-dated money. The monk took from one heap the price the farmer had asked at the fair and handed it to him, saying in reply to questions: 'There are caverned warriors preserved by the good genius of England until that eventful day when, distracted by internecine broils, England shall be thrice lost and won between sunrise and sunset. Then we, awakening from our sleep, shall rise to turn the fate of Britain. This shall be when George the son of George shall reign, when the forests of Delamere shall wave their arms over the slaughtered sons of Albion. Then shall the eagle drink the blood of princes from their headless corpse. Now hasten thee home, for it is not in thy time that these things shall be. A Cestrian shall speak of it and be believed.'

It was not in his time but it is not true that much of that prophecy has been brought to pass? When 'George son of George' was on the throne did not this country find itself lost and won again and again? The fate of Britain was turned by forces outside our knowledge.

So in countless places in his kingdom rests Arthur, the Keltic Messiah, until his country calls him, when he is ever ready to arise with his knights to help her in her need. And has he never risen? Of course he has – again and again. For who is St George of Merrie England? Was it necessary for the hagiologists to unearth an obscure and doubtfully traditional saint from Cappadocia to become the patron saint of the Holy Land of the West? What is George but Arthur Latinized? What are the Georgics but the songs of the husbandmen? Arthur is the Workman or Gardener and George is the Cultivator. When the monks came and the land was slowly made Christian it became necessary in the eyes of the Church to remove the cult of Arthur the Sun God and the Warrior and so Arthur the King was transformed into George the Saint. But the old monks were far too wise to try and break the kingly tradition that had come from an age so much older than their own. As ever when they brought in the new religion they did as their forebears had done before them, and they compromised with the old and kept the great gods in a new guise. They changed a crown into a halo and gave the King a new name but he was still the Arthur that the common people knew and loved. Arthur the King, our own Messiah, is still with us, still holding the safety of the land between his hands, still unsheathing his great sword in the defence of the helpless and the oppressed.

It must not be forgotten that Arthur did not become an 'historical' person till as late as the sixth century AD when Geoffrey of Monmouth wrote down his story and gave it as a history, which Nennius copied from two centuries later. But until he was so pinned down and bounded he was still the traditional King-Priest, Arthur of the Cycles, his story ever the same yet ever varying in details throughout the land as the people told the old tales to their children and grandchildren. And when he passed, as he had to do, with him passed also the power of Merlin the archpriest and of Morgan le Fay, the sister-queen. The passing of Arthur had to be; it was the end of that cycle of evolution – his work as the Third of that early Trinity was over – but he has lived for ever in the hearts of his people, whether they have known him or not, and he waits only to come to their help again when the need is great.

'Childe Rowland to the Dark Tower came.' What then is the Dark Tower? Is it not Caer Sidi, the abode of the perfected ones, four-cornered with a dark door on the shelving side of a hill – the Castle of the Tomb.

And if that is Caer Sidi, where then is the magic cauldron, the British Grail? That is said to lie hidden in Caer Pedryvan, which is always placed 'on the other side of the river', which is the accepted phrase for the Underworld. The Grail and the Cauldron are and must be one and the same and it is necessary for the follower of the Western Tradition to assimilate this fact, for once it has been accepted it is simple to see how everything falls into place. There is Keridwen's Cauldron but earlier still there is Bran's Cauldron; if a slain man were placed in this he was restored to life. Both Cauldron and Grail repel the unworthy, heal the sick and give 'uplift' to the soul. When Arthur descends into Hades to fetch the Cauldron from its dark resting place, he is only conforming to the requirements demanded of all initiates – that he shall perfect his knowledge of spiritual things by descending into the darkness whence he came. It is the parallel of the Descent into Egypt – of Joseph, of Moses and later of Jesus. It is the parallel of the captivity of Daniel when he learnt the ancient Wisdom in the exiled years.

Synesius, once a Bishop of Alexandria, said 'The phantastic spirit may be purified so that something better may be induced; how much then will not the regressing of the rational soul be therefore base, if she neglects to restore that which is foreign to her nature and leaves lingering upon earth that which rightly belongs on high? Since it is possible, by labour and a transition into other lives, for the imaginative soul to be purified and to emerge from this dark abode. And this restoration indeed one or two may obtain as a gift of divinity and initiation.'

'To study the Grail Legend', said Loomis, 'is to dig down through the ruins of buried cities, to uncover layer after layer of extinct civilizations, and forgotten religions.'

Malory and Tennyson did their best or their worst to fix in the minds of their respective generations an Arthur who was a good King but something of an innocent at home. That is not the Arthur of our tradition, the Arthur of our inner knowledge. It is no more true than it is true to think of Merrie England as a gay country with St George of Cappadocia as its patron saint. For Merrie does not mean gay; it is from an old German word which means Fairy. Merrie England was Fairyland or – later – Maryland. It was the Holy Land of the West and its shores were guarded by the Merriemaids or Fairy Girls, daughters of the great Manannan, whom to-day we call Mermaids.

Chapter 4

Merlin and Morgan
and Bride

When one thinks of Arthur, one thinks of Merlin, since he is inextricably bound up with the saga. How does Merlin figure in the Western Mystery Tradition? He is the man from the sea, the man drawn from the primordial water, the first source of all life, who is the wielder of the force on the inner planes where Arthur is the outward and visible sign of the kingship.

Merlin is the wise man, the sage, the Initiator. It is into his hand that the child Arthur is delivered and it is he who superintends his upbringing. He is the British Thoth, the source of all wisdom through whom was transmitted the science of God.

The story of Merlin and Vivien is one of the stories based on the old truths; it is capable of more than one interpretation. The oldest known version in writing appears to be that of Robert de Borron. In this Vivien is called Vivilian, which is a name far more probable than the Norman Vivien to which she was afterwards adjusted. Vivilian represents the fairy beauty for which Merlin is for ever searching. Merlin himself in this story is the son of a fairy man married to a mortal woman; Vivilian is the daughter of a fairy married to a mortal man – a nobleman of Brittany. Merlin lives in Northumberland – that stronghold of the Druidic cult – with his tutor, Blaise, and he and Vivilian meet once every year on Midsummer Eve. Again in this story it is the woman who tempts the man, for Vivilian desires to know the Magic Word which will enable her to raise the Magic Stone which guards the entrance to the Fairy Hills, the domain of the Sidhe. There is no evil in Vivilian in this story; she is ever young and ever beautiful and her curiosity is the curiosity of the innocent. Reluctantly Merlin teaches her the word; she raises the stone, and he and she depart into Fairyland to perpetual enchantment.

Merlin is not the rather cantankerous old magician of some of the more modern versions, growing angry, losing his temper and waving his staff in the air; properly interpreted these are all part of the work of the magician in forming his magic; they are the outward symbols of the power of the magus; the fully directed force with the power of concentration behind him. To the early Kelts Merlin symbolized Wisdom.

Tennyson did him a grave disservice when he wrote Vivien in the *Idylls of the King.* And yet under the rather trite story of the old man cozened by the young witch there is the fundamental truth which must be remembered. Vivien can be taken as the symbol of the new form of belief which was coming in; each new dispensation means the dispersing of the power of the former one.

Vivien is young and Merlin is old; she shuts him up and destroys his power; her name stands for life and living and vitality; she is the strength of the new age.

When Merlin yields to Vivien his work is done, and it matters little whether he be incarcerated in a rock or in a fairy hill or whether he disappears into his glass house, for the intention is the same.

The glass house is the eternal symbol for translation to the inner planes. Some hold that Merlin departed into a glass castle on the Isle of Bardsey off the Welsh coast – a place where many of the most important Druid rites were celebrated. In some old Welsh legends he is said to have departed with eleven comrades in a boat on a sea of glass. This is quoted in the *Triads* as one of the Three Great Losses of Wales.

There is another story that he and his nine ranks of bards all went into a cave on Dinas Emrys – the holy place of Snowdon – taking with them the Thirteen Treasures of Britain. Merlin caused the cave to close by magic but near the entrance he placed a bell which will ring when a 'certain fair youth' approaches, and will then cause the entrance to open and guide the youth to the spot. In the cave he will recover all the books of Merlin and learn his wisdom.

In most of the legends Merlin is stated to have taken with him the Thirteen Treasures. Amongst these was the Mwys, the dish or vessel which was the Grail of the earliest mysteries and clearly corresponds to the Cauldron of Keridwen, for it is stated of it that 'though all the world should approach it, thrice nine men at a time, they would find in it all the food each liked best' and its contents were never exhausted. Another of the Thirteen Treasures was the mantle of King Arthur (occasionally referred to as the 'tartan') which was called King of Light and rendered him invisible.

The glass fortress is mentioned in Nennius, who says 'When certain warriors were sailing from Spain to Ireland there appeared to them in the middle of the sea a tower of glass, the summit of which appeared covered with men, to whom they often spoke but received no answer. They besieged the tower but when they landed on the shore at its base the sea opened and swallowed them up.' In the *Book of the Dun Cow* Cuchullin tells of a similar magic tower, the fort of Scatha, a Caledonian witch, which had within it a magic cauldron and gold and silver treasure. Norse mythology tells of a glass heaven called Glerhiminn, and Taliesin reports:

> Beyond the Glass Fort Arthur's valour they had not seen;
> Three score hundreds stood on the wall;
> It was hard to converse with their watchman.

But Merlin is also an historic person; the name is generic and was usually given to a Bard of much power and seniority. In the sixth century AD there was a Merlin called a Bard who was described four hundred years later by another Bard as 'the supreme judge of the North, president of Bardic Lore about the waters of the Clyde'. He taught the mysteries as they had been taught at Stonehenge and he was himself called 'the Caledonian' and 'the Swineherd'.

It is considered possible that there were two historic Merlins apart from the legendary but none the less real magi; Merlin ap Morvyn and Merlin Ambrosius appear in the records as being brought before Vortigern in AD 480 and Merlin Ambrosius at the court of Rydderch Hael in 570, when he was an old man. Merlin Ambrosius probably was patronized by Ambrosius, brother of Uther Pendragon, father of Arthur; in these two brothers we have once again the eternal duality; the twins, Ambrosius (which means

Immortal or Spiritual) and Pendragon, the fighting Dragon, the active partner.

The reference to Merlin as a swineherd brings into focus one of the more important of the Keltic mythological illusions. The sacred animal of the Keridwen worship is the Great White Sow, which is her personification just as the Cow is that of Isis-Hathor. The inner symbology of the story is illustrated by the legend that in her Sow form Keridwen would fly over Wales and Ireland and that from time to time she dropped her litter on to the land. And wherever she dropped her offspring a mystery school sprang up. It is an interesting possibility to carry this idea up to the present time and remember the common saying 'Pigs can't fly'. Nor could the piglings, for they were the neophytes, the young priests, and it was only the Mother, the great White Sow herself from whom the new mystery schools could emanate.

Shakespeare knew of this symbology when he wrote *The Merchant of Venice*, a play which is full of allusion, chiefly through the meaning of the names of his characters. He calls his heroine Portia which, being interpreted literally, is the Sow. In that play he has pictured her as sitting upon her throne in her castle at Belmont, the ever beautiful Mountain of Attainment; Wisdom sits upon the hill and from there she, as the heavenly Sophia, is appealed to by men to resolve their difficulties. The names of the characters in most of Shakespeare's plays, other than the strictly historical ones, are full of symbolic meaning, and it is hardly to be doubted but that his contemporaries would have known what he meant and the inferences and lessons he was attempting to draw for the initiated.

According to the *Mabinogion*, one of Arthur's occupations was the pursuit of wild pigs. According to one of the stories in that volume the White Sow as Henwen or Keridwen dropped the germs of wealth for Britain in her journeyings – three grains of wheat, three honey bees, a grain of barley, a piglet and a grain of rye. It is instructive to note that the first two are elsewhere recorded as the gifts of the Lords of an earlier Evolution who brought them to mankind from another sphere and came to the land of Chaldea. Unfortunately, Keridwen also decided to leave three troublesome children in the world – perhaps to give needed opposition and prevent stagnation – for she dropped a wolf cub, an eaglet and a kitten, all of whom caused much distress; in their time, especially the kitten, which grew up to be known as the Palug Cat, one of the Three Plagues of Mona or Angelsey.

It is interesting to compare the Keltic legends with the parable of the Prodigal Son. He, it will be remembered, also went out of his father's house – which has been interpreted as going down the arc of evolution into matter. He, too, at his lowest ebb became a swineherd; to the Jews this was the lowest form of employment, but with the inner meaning of the parable in its translation into English, it is also the story of how he found the heavenly wisdom in incarnation and returned to his father's palace in heaven. It is the story of the man who lost all to find all.

There is a legend too that Mary Magdalene lies buried in Iona. She roamed the world after the Crucifixion in company with a blind man, but there was no sin in their association. One day, wandering the hills of Scotland, she came to Knoidart where she and her companion rested. But her first husband, who had never given up the search for her, tracked her thither and she knew that he would kill the blind man. So she instructed him to lie down among a herd of swine, so that he was concealed by them and she herself stood by as the herdwife. But as she was keeping her watch, her husband caught up with her and laughed. 'That is a fine boar you have there', he said and thrust his spear through the heart of the blind man, so that he died upon the instant. Then he proceeded to cut off the beautiful hair of Mary and left her, weeping ceaselessly until she died. One of Columba's monks found her wandering and crying upon the hillside, and took her in a boat to Iona, where she lived the rest of her life. When she died, she was buried in a cave but none but Columba ever knew her for who she was.

It has been said that basically this is but another version of Diarmaid and Grania, the eternal love story. But it is possible and permissible to see it as another example of the deep symbolism of our Western Tradition. Love, we know, is blind, and man is blind upon the inner plane where he is negative and woman is positive. He is seeking her wisdom and she, the eternal mother, is protecting him. Comes the world, in the shape of the indignant husband. The eternal mother tries to save her son by hurriedly hiding him among the priests and neophytes; but he is not ready for the teaching of the spirit and he is spiritually slain by the cares of the world. Even the priestess cannot control the blind passions and desires of the uninitiated; there is a time when the teaching of the spirit can prevail and a time when it cannot.

And when the 'evil days' come and the Word of God is driven underground by the material thinking of the world, then the great Mother is shorn of her glory, her hair, for that is the symbol of her strength and her supremacy.

And so Merlin is called a swineherd, meaning that he was the master of a mystery school. In a poem attributed to him he speaks of the wonderful orchard which contained the secret of earth and of planetary revolution, revealed to him by his own master, the Hierophant Gwendolleu, who is also called sometimes Prydydd Mawr, or the Great Bard.

> 'To no one has been exhibited at one hour of dawn (that is to say, the hour of initiation) what was shown to Merddyn before he became aged; namely seven score and seven delicious apple trees of equal age, height, length and size, which spring from the bosom of Mercy. One white bending veil covers them over ... The delicious apple trees, with blossoms of pure white and wide spreading branches, produce sweet apples for those who can digest them. And they have always grown in the wood which grows apart ...' (that is the Sanctuary of the Mysteries.)

The key to this mystery is the number of the apple trees (one hundred and forty-seven). It is the square of the perfect seven multiplied by the mystical three and it refers to the sevenfold system of world evolution in co-operation with the Trinity.

This wonderful orchard was guarded by two dusky birds who each wore a yoke of gold. These birds correspond to the Ravens of Odin and to the two horns which Moses wore upon his forehead. In other words they were the two wings or petals seen by a clairvoyant spectator when the clairvoyant eye is being used by the seer. They are of course the immediate information that the orchard is not to be found on this plane but is only in the inner vision.

The Ravens are the representation of the pupils in the Mystery School, who helped to guard the orchard and acted as assistants to the priests. The whole of the poem from which this short quotation is taken goes on to tell of the loss of these clairvoyant powers as the intellect took over from the intuition during the process of evolution.

M. de Villemarque has translated a poem from the Breton which has come down from the very early days.

> Merlin, Merlin, where art thou going
> So early in the day with thy black dog?
> I have come here to search for the way,
> To find the red egg;
> The red egg of the marine serpent,
> By the seaside in the hollow of the stone.
> I am going to seek in the valley
> The green water cress and the golden grass
> And the top branch of the oak,
> In the wood by the side of the fountain.
> Merlin, Merlin, retrace your steps;
> Leave the branch on the oak
> And the green water cress in the valley
> As well as the golden grass;
> And leave the red egg of the marine serpent
> In the foam by the hollow of the stone.
> Merlin! Merlin! Retrace thy steps
> There is no diviner but God.

M. de Villemarque says that 'golden grass' is a medicinal plant greatly valued by the peasant Bretons. If a man tread on it, he will fall asleep and will understand the language of animals and birds. It has to be gathered from the root and not cut, the gatherer being barefoot, fasting and clad in a white robe; no iron must be employed; the right hand should be passed under the left arm and the linen of the robe should only be used once.

As can clearly be seen, it is based on a powerful incantation of the Druid times and Christianized by the addition of the last verse, when Merlin is reminded that his age has passed.

The red egg of the marine sea-serpent suggests the famous 'adders' eggs' of the Druids of which more will be found in another chapter. Water cress is a water weed and had probable clairvoyant properties; it was connected with the magic world of the water in which it grew. The top branch of the oak is probably allusion to the mistletoe which was cut from the highest possible branch on which it grew, while the wood is the sacred oak grove or temple of the Druids beside the symbolical water of truth.

Merlin is therefore the wise man and the scribe and the priest of the Western tradition. He it is who came first bringing the knowledge of Atlantis and he it is who shall surely waken our hearts and our inner knowledge to receive our heritage anew. For the mystery of our religion remains, whatever its outward and visible form. The basis of the mysteries is still the same, whether the presiding form be called a Bishop or a Druid or a Magus. The great magicians of our past, the great wizards of our history, are all lineal descendants in power of the first embryonic Merlin, the man who rose from the deep waters.

The late Mr W. L. Courtney once said

> 'Christianity is a great mystery religion; it is THE Mystery Religion. Its priests are called to an awful and tremendous hierurgy; its pontiffs are to be the pathfinders, the bridge makers between the world of senses and the world of spirit. And, in fact, they pass their time in preaching, not the eternal mysteries, but a two-penny morality, in changing the Wine of Angels and the Bread of Heaven into ginger-beer and mixed biscuits; a sorry transubstantiation, a sad alchemy, as it seems to me.'

So far down in our time as the sixth century the Druid view is clearly laid out in the fourteenth verse of the *Ode of Varieties*, (Myvyrian Vol. 1.)

> Out of the holy wheaten grain
> And the red generous wine
> Is constructed the mysterious body
> Of Christ, son of Alpha.

Alpha is Elphin, the king who rescued the child Taliesin when he was thrown into the river by his mother Keridwen, and here the Druids have simply substituted the new name for the old. There is but one Holy Child in whatever pantheon he may dwell. As the old Cornish proverb has it – A dear child has many names.

And after Merlin – Morgan. Of her there is little that we can say, for she is ever the hidden one, the shadowy woman who stands behind, giving of her power from the inner planes. She is the feminine principle of the great Triangle of King, Priest and Priestess; she is the Word, the life-giving Force. She is the Spirit of God, the third person of the Trinity who is or should always be feminine – the Ruach of the Hebrew, the Sophia of Greece, Wisdom that sits upon her seven hills.

Morgan is she who teaches men to work with power; she is Binah on the Tree of Life; the great Mother of form through whom is the manifestation of force.

She is the third of the three shadowy Queens, the old Queen, the Queen-sister of the King, and it is she who takes his head upon her knees in the last journey down to Avalon.

She is also Isis of the Moon, and her place on the Tree of Life can be in Yesod, for in the later pantheon she is changed into Arianrhod. Like all women, she is all things and her aspects are infinite. The Church was afraid of Morgan and left her alone; contenting itself with calling her the Witch-woman. But always she draws us back to the primordial sea from which she came, to the old mysteries of Atlantis, whence our own have derived their life; she is that strange and lovely lady whom we can sometimes glimpse on a rocky seashore, rising out of the water, shadowy in the sea mist and the foam. She has all wisdom and all knowledge.

And the third great person we have to remember in considering those of the old gods who have come down to us is Bride or Brigit. She was, you will remember, a daughter of the Dagda; the transition from goddesshood to sainthood was for her the easiest of things.

She was herself a triple goddess, the beloved of the North and whether she be St Bridget or St Bride she is still the heart love of the true Kelt – the darling saint as she was the darling goddess.

Originally she was a sun goddess or a fire goddess; all the little attributes we know of her go to prove this. The story goes that she was born at sunrise; a house in which she dwelt burst into a flame that reached up to heaven. When she took the veil as a nun before her sanctification it is reported that a pillar of fire rose from her head – a simple enough transference from a fire goddess. Life-giving was she too, for her breath could raise the dead – true symbol of the sun, the source of all life.

It was because of this simplicity of transition, no doubt, that she has always held her place in the hearts of the peasants. Not for them to understand the difference in religion when the Christian Church brought in its teaching; they might accept what they could not argue with, but at least they kept their darling goddess, even if they now called her a Saint, and she listened to their prayers in her new robe as she had done in the old one. They could still continue to invoke her without incurring the wrath of the new priests and it was an easy thing to settle down to the new regime.

The sacred flame on her shrine at Kildare was never allowed to go out. Every nineteen days it was tended by the nuns who served her, and every twentieth day it burnt of its own accord. Once in the thirteenth century an accident occurred and the flame was extinguished, but except for that moment it remained alight till the suppression of the monasteries by Henry VIII. The fire goddess was honoured even when her origin had been forgotten.

As a triple goddess, Bride or Brigit was the Goddess of Poetry, the Goddess of Healing and the Goddess of Smithcraft – not one would think a very expected subject for her patronage. But if the fire of the forge be remembered then it is highly suitable for a goddess of fire to be served by the smiths.

In Gaelic Scotland they spoke of her as Bride of the Golden Hair, Bride of the White Hills, Mother of the King of Glory, and in mediaeval Ireland she was known also as 'Mary of the Gael', showing how blended the two forms of worship had become. For Bride is the triad, young and virgin, mature in her beauty and then the mother who is also the slayer since she brings forth life which is death.

In the Hebrides, her own islands, whose name is now mispronounced, she is called Muime Chrioso – the Foster-Mother of Christ. And she is also Bride the Milkmaid, the young moon goddess akin to Isis Hathor and all the other goddesses of that rank. There is an old Hebridean rann or chanty addressed to the cattle of which one verse runs in the translation of Fiona Macleod:

> The Protection of God and Columba
> Encompass your going and coming,
> And about you be the milkmaid of the smooth white palms,
> Brigit of the golden hair, clustering brown.

It is said there also that St Bride's Flower, St Bride's Bird and St Bride's Gift make a fine spring and a good year. Her flower is the dandelion, of the bright gold of the sun; her bird is the oyster catcher, and her gift is the cradle – for Bride presides over childbirth and a birth in spring is good luck for both mother and babe. Bride's own day is the first of February, the eve of Candlemas in the Christian Church – and in her own islands she was greeted by the women in their special manner. A sheaf of oats from the last harvest was dressed in girl's clothing and laid in a basket with a club of wood, representing the male opposite. Then the basket was lifted by the women and carried round the village while they cried 'Bride is come! Bride is come! Bride is in the bed!', welcoming in this way the goddess of the new spring.

One of the best known shrines to Bride in the West Country was that of Beckary near Glastonbury. The land round there is still called Brigit's Isle or Little Ireland, Beg-Eri. There it was that Arthur the King had his vision of the Mother of God when she appeared to him as he knelt upon the green grass and gave him a great crystal cross, which became later the property of the Abbot of Glastonbury. It was after that time, according to the legends, that Arthur fought no longer under the shield of the Red Dragon – which is even to-day the flag of Wales – but under his own device of a crystal cross on a green ground.

In parts of England Bride was worshipped as the goddess of poetry right up to the Puritan days, her healing powers being invoked also by poetic incantations at sacred wells. One of the best known of these was that of Bridewell in London, which, though later a prison, started as a hospital or place of healing.

In his book *The White Goddess*, Robert Graves has pointed out that 'there is an unconscious hankering in Britain after goddesses, if not for a goddess as dominant as the original triple goddess, at least for a female softening of the all-maleness of the Christian Trinity.' The Church, by representing the Holy Ghost as a Dove and never suggesting the femininity of the aspect, has done a great disservice both to itself and to the world in general. The Perfect Trinity must have an eternal female to balance the eternal male, both begotten and proceeding. There must be the mother of all living to stand at the head of the left hand pillar of the Tree. The word Spirit comes from the Hebrew feminine. So this place has been to some extent 'usurped' by the Mother of Jesus, who is indeed the personification of the Spirit on the plane of matter, and who should be regarded as the counterpart of the Eternal Son in His human form; for, as we are told quite clearly by the Apostle Paul, 'The letter killeth but the spirit giveth life'. There is no future in the material world, but the spirit which comes down through the left hand pillar of the Tree of Life is immortal, passing through the spheres till it manifests in all the Virgin Goddesses and all the Virgin Mothers. It is the source of that triple goddess who is so peculiarly beloved in this land.

All through the Middle Ages it is the Queen of Heaven and her train of female saints which capture the imagination of the people. In their secret hearts the image of the goddess had never been dispaced. It was this that made it simple for the Church to divert their devotion to the great Mother Goddess to the Mother of God, as Virgin, as Mother and as Mater Dolorosa when she stood by the Cross of Calvary. She was but the old triplicity under a new set of names.

In his edition of the Taliesin poems, D. V. Nash says that the poets of the thirteenth and fourteenth centuries repeatedly refer to the Virgin as the cauldron or source of inspiration; for them the Goddess and the cauldron were interchangeable; to this they were led by one of those plays upon words so dear to the mediaeval litterati; in Keltic *pair* stands for a cauldron and in its secondary form it becomes *mair*, which is also Mary. Mary was therefore Mair the Mother of Jesus, the mystical receptacle of the Holy Spirit, and Pair was the cauldron or receptacle of Christian inspiration. In the thirteenth century Davydd Benfras wrote in one of his poems of 'Christ, son of Mary, my cauldron of pure descent'.

When Henry VIII destroyed the old religion and suppressed the numerous monasteries and convents dedicated to Our Lady, what he was really doing by describing himself as Head of the Church was trying to destroy the worship of the goddess, which was inherent in the land, and to substitute for it the worship of the god, personified by himself. In other countries, Kings are the fathers of their people, but in this country it is the Queen who holds the unconscious devotion and it is under her Queens that this country knows success.

When Elizabeth Tudor came to the throne she was acclaimed by the common people because she was to them the new representation of the goddess; her very Tudor liveries of white and green were the symbols of the young May Queen and the new birth of Bride. Even her hair was the colour of fire and the sun. The names which her people bestowed on her proclaimed their belief in her as the re-creation of their eternal mother, for all her names are those of the Moon Goddess – Phoebe, Virginia, Gloriana – in the fullness of her splendour. Men died for her because they found in her the object of their hidden and instinctive devotion. They went round the world braving danger and disaster to bring glory to her as the ruler of the land; they endured her caprices, her stinginess, her utter lack of outward support for their ventures as part of the natural characteristics of the goddess. 'O swear not by the moon, th' inconstant moon!' Yet by the moon men have ever sworn their vows to their ladies.

And for her part Elizabeth remained unwedded, as the goddess should do; for whom the goddess takes as her lover dies in the fullness of the moontide.

If the struggles between Elizabeth Tudor and Mary Stuart be stripped down to their essentials it will be seen that they were actually a series of struggles between the two triple goddesses in deadly feud. It was the last phase of the fight for it was the end of the division between the three kingdoms of the island. Wales and England had been united and the time had come when there had to be but one personification of the triple goddess throughout the three countries. It was her heritage as the goddess that made the young nobles of Scotland fight and die for Mary; whether they knew it or not she was the embodiment of their deepest devotion.

When not a hundred years later, the bitter war between King and Parliament took place, the banner under which the Cavaliers fought was that of the Virgin, with long streaming hair. They called the Queen Mary and nominally they fought in her defence, but beneath their consciousness was the great subconscious race allegiance and it was the triple goddess whom they were determined to defend against the Puritans who would take all the joy out of this Holy Land of the west.

We have come a long way by now from the gentle Bride of the Hills but she still lives in the hearts of men and women. To her is owed much of the position of women in this country – their freedom, their dignity and the respect accorded to them. Throughout the centuries men have held in their hearts their love of the goddess, whose emblem is the White Swan – that strong and beautiful bird striking out boldly into the unknown north where lie always the hidden mysteries untouched by man.

Chapter 5

The holy Places

To work the Mysteries successfully there must be in all cases a holy place, a consecrated temple, whether it be out of doors in a clearing in the forest, on the summit of a hill open to the four winds of heaven, in a cathedral or within the tiniest of rooms. Consecration can be achieved by the power of thought and the association of ideas; to the one who understands, the material use of the magical weapons is not necessary; they can be visualized upon the inner plane, though it is always advisable if possible to make some definite contact with the material world in which the work is to take place.

A place used for rites and ceremonies throughout the centuries will keep within itself the influence and the power poured into it through the work of those who have used it in the past. This is that 'atmosphere' felt so often by sensitive and even not so sensitive people in certain places – both out of doors and within. The men of knowledge consecrate with a force that is retained, more especially within four walls, and unless the contacts be broken it will linger for an untold time – the time depending on circumstances. These consecrations – which can be for good or for evil – account for a number of the haunted houses of which one hears from time to time; the contacts established and the powers called up are not emptied out of the vessel in which they have been contained.

This means of course that the worker of the same rituals is more easily able to function in a place which has already been used; for the shell, as it were, of the former working is present even if the life of it has apparently departed. That is why such a head of power can be brought up so quickly in a place such as an old chapel or church where the rites have been performed again and again in the same way and for the same end. It is like relighting a flame in a lamp which is still full of oil and waiting only the taper to burst forth again into illumination.

So it is we find among the holy places of Britain homes of such enduring strength that even the least sensitive of us can catch the faint echo of the departed glory, dispersed as it may have been by thousands of the unthinking masses tramping through the sacred aisles.

To put oneself in the attitude of prayer is the first requisite of achieving prayer, was the dictum of St Ignatius Loyola, and it is the case with our own contacts with our secret places; let us be ready to receive, and it will be given to us and we shall find ourselves no more strangers and foreigners but at home in the cradles of our own traditions.

These places are the centres of magical power. Now, magic is a word that has been so much misused in this country and in this language that the ordinary man is usually afraid of it, which is after all just something he does not understand, something which is knowledge transmitted into form on the material plane. Magic, which is the work of the magus or wise man, might best be defined as the knowledge of how to use powers that are not fully comprehended by others; the ability to control natural forces; to work with the superconscious mind deliberately and not with the conscious one; in fact, to make use of the talents which God has given us, which are not all confined to the sphere of matter.

Remember that the magic of one century is the commonplace of another; how else would, for example, radio and television have been described in a less scientific age than our own, had such a magus as Roger Bacon discovered them? Yet we take them in our stride and merely complain if the results on our sets are not of the quality we have been led to expect. If you can transmit a picture from New York to London, why should it be more difficult or more incomprehensible to transmit a picture from the inner planes to the conscious awareness that is then enabled to describe it?

Pliny, who must be taken into account as a serious writer by all students of the Classics, wrote on the Religion of Magic as follows:

Magic is one of the few things it is important to discuss at some length, were it only because, being the most delusive of all the arts, it has everywhere and at all times been most powerfully credited. Nor need it surprise us that it has obtained so vast an influence, for it has united in itself the three arts which have wielded the most powerful sway over the spirit of man. Springing in the first instance from Medicine – a fact which no one can doubt – and under cover of a solicitude for our health, it has glided into the mind and taken the form of another medicine, more holy and more profound. In the second place, bearing the most deceptive and flattering promises, it has enlisted the motive of Religion, the subject about which even to this day mankind is most in the dark. To crown all, it has had recourse to Astrology; and every man is eager to know the future and convinced that this knowledge is most certainly to be obtained from the heavens. Thus, holding the minds of men enchained in the triple bond, it has extended its sway over many nations and the Kings of Kings obey it in the East.

Much later, in 1531, Cornelius Agrippa, secretary and librarian to Margaret of Parma at Louvain, defended the practice of magic in his *De Occulta Philosophia*.

Where then is what might be considered the chief centre of magical worship in the Western Tradition? Not, as some might think, at Stonehenge, powerful though that centre was and is, but at Glastonbury, as it is always called to-day. Here throughout the ages had been the centre of our teaching; known of old as the Isle of Avalon, the Isle of Apples, called in the Keltic Inis Vitrin, the Shining Isle, Glastonbury was old and wise in the Mysteries long before Joseph of Arimathea came with the Holy Grail, long before the legend that on an earlier merchant's journey he brought with him the Holy Child, who played among the tin mines of the Mendips.

For Avalon is the secret Garden of the Hesperides, the Garden where the sacred apples grew watched over by nine fair maidens – the Garden immortalized for ever for our younger generations in the story of Jason and the Argonauts in their search for the Golden Fleece. The inner significance of the story of the Argo and of the Fleece is far too great and vast for it to be entered upon here but it well repays study by those who are not yet conversant with its symbolism. The nine maidens represent the triple divisions of the triple Goddess, herself the original triplicity of the One, and the Muses are but her varying aspects. The circle of maidens with joined hands is the outer protection of the apple tree; while the serpent of Wisdom lies coiled around its trunk, tail in mouth, representing the unending circle of Eternity and the mystic phrase 'In my end is my beginning'.

In the Keltic mythology it is that apple which is the sacred fruit, a talisman which led people to the land of the gods and provided them with life and love and joy. Apollo is reckoned to have been its personification in god form, and according to Dr Rendel Harris and other authorities the word Apollo was originally Apellon, which has been described as a 'loan word' from the north, for the Apple only reached Greece by way of the north and its original name is still the Keltic 'abal'.

It is the poisoned apple representing false knowledge and the misuse of it which nearly kills Snow White in the fairytale; it is the Apple of Discord which sets off the Trojan War; it is the Apple of Wisdom which William Tell, so much personified in his native country and now so doubtfully of any historical origin at all, has to shoot from the head of his son. True wisdom demands only the best from its seekers and devotees; it demands unerring aim and purest concentration. The William Tell story is to be found also in the Wayland Saga, another great part of our heritage, when Egil, Wayland's brother, has to shoot the apple from the head of his son Orandel, at the court of Nithiad, thereby to win favour and safety for himself and his family.

The sacred drink of the Druids was La Mas Ushal (pronounced Lambswool) and this was made from roasted apples, sugar and ale. It was especially brewed at the end of October, 1 November being dedicated to the god presiding over fruits, seeds and so forth – the time of the preparation of the soil for the forthcoming sowing and the beginning of the winter season when the germination took place in the quiet dark. It is a point worth noticing, perhaps, that the Druids called November the first Mas Ushal, the day of the apple, and it does not take an undue amount of imagination to see how the Church later translated it into All Souls and established it as the feast of the dead, resting before the Second Coming of Spring.

Let us consider this land of Avalon, set deep in the heart of the west of England yet not so deep as to be entirely inaccessible. It was in the Summer Land, at the end of Paradise, and it was an island when the waters of the Brue and the neighbouring streams flowed over their low banks before the marshes were drained and the rhines cut. Then in the flood days the only dry land was the Tor and the little path over the lower hills to Wearyall where once a pilgrim hut was built. On what is now called Chalice Hill by the side of the Tor it is said that Morgan le Fay once dwelt and presided over the Well of Sacrifice. It is a strange Well, with sides of dressed stone cut in great blocks and unlike any of the stone of the neighbourhood, where the water is always ice cold, whatever the temperature of the day, and tinged with red as with the blood of the sacrifice, and where the niche for the offering is cut out of the wall. Every so often the water flows freely and the level of the Well rises, and at these magic moments the man chosen for the sacrifice was set bound within the niche that by his death the will of the Gods might be known.

Tradition has it that at this same time the Tor was crowned with a circle of stones, for it was, like Stonehenge, an open Temple of the Sun, and the graded way to the top was the processional route of the priests, though it is now called the Pilgrim Way. And I will myself vouch for the fact that strange things happen on the Tor when no human being is present; that there are times and seasons when the Old Gods still hold their sway and none but their servants are permitted to walk the processional way. I have myself in all innocence attempted to climb the Tor in the summer evening light and have been inexorably but gently forced back by some unseen power, not inimical, not hurrying nor urgent, but indicating in no uncertain terms that that which was to be done was secret and that intruders were to be dissuaded. There were others with me that evening and we were all conscious of the same power in varying degrees and none of us was free from it till we had gone back through the small gate on to the lower slopes.

What would have happened had we insisted on going on, I have no idea; one has manners in occult work as in everything else, and having been told so clearly that it was none of our business it would have been the greatest rudeness to have insisted on continuing.

What constitutes the magic of Avalon if it is not symbolized by the flooded land of still water, the magic mirror, with the tall finger of the Tor rising above it as the magician's wand of power, and in the middle the little island where the Apples of Wisdom grew?

Before the advent of the Christian era there were many other holy places in Britain besides Avalon, but not all of them were taken over and transformed into shrines of the new religion. The second most holy place of the Keltic faith was Great Orme's Head of Anglesey. The Isle of Anglesey, or Mona, was called Inis or Ynys Dywyal, or the Dark Isle, because of the shade of the enormous groves of oak trees which grew upon it, forming the open-to-the-sky temples of the Druids. It is the opposite of Ynys Vitrin, the Isle of Light, for here the Mysteries were worked in the deep shadows. The Great Orme itself is but a variation of the Great Worm or Serpent and the contours of the country show how the convolutions of the snake may be traced. It is the other great aspect of the serpent worship opposed in the sense of being opposite to that of the Serpent in the Garden of the Golden Apples.

Here, then, may be found the inevitable and essential pair of opposites – the Shining Isle and the Dark Isle. But there must always be three to form the Trinity of Power. Where then is the sacred third that corresponds to Avalon and Great Orme's Head – with which they must be united in the form of the triangle?

Draw a line from one to the other and use that as the base of a triangle, projecting each of the other sides from the two centres till they meet equilaterally. And where do they meet? In the western sea off the coast of Ireland. There, so tradition has it, lies the third and most holy centre of the Western Mysteries, so holy, so withdrawn that it has not yet descended into matter but leads us ever to contemplate its glory in the sunset sky.

It has been glimpsed from time to time by those who have the vision. It is seen in the glory of the dying sun on the horizon, and the men of old called it Hy Brazil – the Island of the Red Light. Hi is the corruption of He or Hu, the sun god, as well as the generic word for island, and the land of Hy Brazil symbolized him in his aspect of the setting sun, for Brazil was the name of a red wood dye.

All through the ages the mysterious island has been the dream of mankind; it is the Golden Land of the West, the land of the tired warriors, the ultima thule of the traveller and the sailor.

So deeply was it graven in the hearts of men that the memory of it stayed with them throughout the centuries and the old charts mark it as a genuine place, about a hundred miles west of County Clare.

From the year 1424 to 1467 it was marked on the so-called Venetian Map and other charts as being somewhere west of the Azores. In his journal for 9 April, 1492, Columbus notes that the inhabitants of Hierro, Comera and Madeira have seen it in the west, and in that same year Martin Behaim of Wurtemburg also placed it off the Azores. Naturally this strange and unknown island fired the imagination; it was sufficiently authenticated to be marked on the charts and yet no one could be found who had landed there; in the two centuries between 1526 and 1721 no fewer than four expeditions were fitted out and sent to locate it. But in 1759 the scientists came to the conclusion that it was a trick of the light, a mirage created by certain recurrent cloud effects at sunset in certain atmospheric circumstances.

But throughout the ages the story of the fo'c'sle has been that the island lies off the west coast of Ireland. Traditionally in the early Irish legends it was said to have been discovered by St Brandan, the companion of St Patrick. But St Brandan is only the Christianized version of Bran, god of the underworld, and it would be natural that he should be given the responsibility of discovering such an island. It is strictly in keeping with its mythical and mystical origin that it should be in St Brandan's care. Indeed the two statements hang together to make the whole. St Brandan is reputed to have sailed on a miraculous voyage to Hy Brazil and to have died there – a piece of natural symbolism that needs no explanation. The traditional date of this voyage is between AD 565 and 575 and the oldest extant version of it in writing is the eleventh century MS called *Navigatia Brandoni*. Here the island is called the Promised Land of Saints and the Golden Island of the West, and one of its legendary attributes is that there no man grows old and none knows sorrow. It is only another location for Tir n' an Oige.

We have but to consider the various references in our own

time to 'going West' when leaving this world to realize how deeply this myth of our heritage has sunk into our subconscious selves. Even in the lighter verse of one of our modern poets who understood the call of the old gods we have the same idea ... 'Follow the gipsy patteran, West of the sinking sun ... Morning waits at the end of the world And the world is all at our feet.' It is the same island to which Charles Kingsley sent the good Water Babies on Sundays – St Brandan's Fairy Isle which they found as a foretaste of heaven.

There is nothing in the mystery teaching of our race which is incompatible with belief in this fairy island of the west which has not yet descended into matter – and indeed may never do so – where the Blessed have passed to a life beyond our knowledge.

In Miss Katherine M. Buck's translation of *The Wayland Saga* the same allusions occur. The three fairy brides of the three heroes, Wayland and his brothers, after years of happy married life, find their original wild swan feathered skins and, putting them on, turn back into swans and make their way to their old haunts in the West.

So flew they south o'er Mirkwood, then due west,
O'er the swans' bath setting their swift course,
And came ere thrice the sun had girdled earth
Unto the Western Isles of Mystery ...
The secret Island where they fain would be ...
Somewhere beyond the Faroe Isles these lie,
But where is known to none of mortal birth.
Some sail there in their dreams and stay awhile
But when they wake, their tongues refuse to tell
What they have seen, and soon fades quite away
From most men's minds the distant memory
Of those fair Islands of strange Fantasy;
They have no chart ... forgotten is the way
By which they reached that country ... all is lost.'

To reach the Islands of the Blessed one must have a boat of some kind and the Irish stories have many references to the crystal or glass canoes in which the heroes sail away out of mortal ken. This is the traditional symbolic reference to a change of plane, of

a transition from this material life to the inner one of the spirit.
Connla the Red was spirited away to Fairyland in a glass boat;
Taliesin the Bard says that Alexander the Great went on invisible
voyages, and in one of the great Keltic poems it is said that 'the
multitude could not see the hero's progress after he had entered
his glass vessel'. The same idea prevails in the story of Cinderella.
The key to that story is the glass slipper; when she wears that
Cinderella is transported to the place where she really belongs, at
the side of her Prince. Even her name is a clue to the mystery
significance of the story, for Ella is a variation of Ellen or Helen,
the oldest feminine name in the world, meaning Light. Cinderella
is but Light Obscured and when she is transported into her natural
medium on the inner planes she is radiantly clothed and recognized
as a princess, even though none knows her name.

So much for the first great triangle of power.

There was a second great triangle which came into being after
the Christian Church had taken hold of the country. As has been
pointed out before, the Church built wherever possible on the
foundations laid by its predecessors; they turned Arthur into a Saint
and they took the holy place of Glastonbury and diverted its channel
of power so that it became that of the new dispensation. Now it is
that Glastonbury becomes the great centre of the Christian worship,
as before it had been the holy of holies of the old gods; now the
Grail becomes the Cup of the Last Supper brought to this country
by Joseph of Arimathea after the Crucifixion; and now it is hidden
by the mysterious Fisher King in Chalice Hill, which was once the
home of Morgan le Fay, and the calm water of the Well of Sacrifice
which was indeed her Chalice becomes Chalice Well but the
meaning thereof is lost to the uninitiated.

The second great triangle of the newer Mysteries is formed by
Glastonbury, Iona and Lindisfarne or Holy Island off the coast of
Northumberland – a triangle that faces east instead of west. This
is a triangle of great potency but of a power that is quite different
from that of the older one. It is necessary that changes should
come and seats of power be varied since as the world progresses
in evolution, the type of power to be worked must be different.
You cannot afford to get your lines mixed when you are working
magic, or the last state of the magician is worse than the first. It is

not wise to work the Christian rituals in the places where the old gods still hold sway.

Glastonbury remains then in both triangles, the link between the old and the new, which has been the cause of its designation as 'the holiest erthe in England'; but in the new order the chief seat of the power is the wattle Church of St Joseph and not the Tor. There the Church carefully built a church and a tower dedicated to St Michael, whose duty it is to keep down the old gods as he threw the bright Lucifer from Heaven; but the church has fallen into disuse and the Tor remains, so that it would seem that he was not as successful as was expected.

Of Iona there is much that could be said and that cannot be said here. It was always a holy place, for God was revered there before Colum came. Both the priests of the sun and the priests of the moon had their temples on Iona. No one knows with certainty who occupied the island before the coming of Colum and his monks, but the legend goes that once a woman was worshipped there – and that was even before the days of moon goddesses. She might have been an ancestral Bride – for Bride is the goddess of the northlands – or she might have been an aspect of Danu or Ana, or even Isis under a new name, brought by the Kelts in their wanderings from the Middle East and Egypt.

As Fiona Macleod has said, 'To tell the story of Iona is to go back to God and to end in God.' As with the stories of Arthur, the founding of the Christian Church and the stories of Columba and his monks are known far and wide and can be read of in detail in many Lives of the Saints and of the early Church and they do not concern us here. But there are some aspects of the early days which are a part of the purpose of this book.

The very name of Iona is uncertain in its origin. Fiona Macleod, after considerable investigation locally, says that in pre-Columba days it was Iouain, and that Iona is but the normal Gaelic pronounciation of Ishona – Island of Saints. He, after prolonged consideration, discards Hy or Hu, the Keltic word for island, as having nothing to do with Innis, which is Gaelic. Iona is also said to mean Island of the Dove – and Columba is also the Dove. The Anglicized Gaelic would be Icolmkill, meaning Isle of Colum of the Church. In 1771 an anonymous Gaelic writer put forward the idea that Christianity was already upon Iona before the coming of Colum and that the island was already dedicated to St John 'for it was originally called I'Eion – the Isle of John – whence Iona'. This is a theory of some interest to us as will be seen in the chapter concerning the possible Keltic origin of St John.

There were no doubt Christian monks before Conall King of Alba (though only Dalriadic King of Argyll) invited Colum to Iona, and among them was Oran or Odrun, who is chronicled as having been a missionary priest and who had died fifteen years before Colum landed. The Arch-Druid was then a Cymric priest called Gwendolleu and he protested through his second Druid, Myrddin, that he no longer dared to practise his rites 'in raised circles' – 'the grey stones themselves even they have removed'. In *Keltic Researches* Davies speaks of Colum having burned a heap of Druidical books, but neither Colum nor Adamnan or other early chroniclers speak of Iona being held by Druids when they arrived. And the name by which they refer to it – Innis nan Druidneachan – might well mean only Isle of Priests. St Adamnan, the Abbot at the end of the seventh century, and ninth in line, calls the island simply Ioua or Iouan Island.

In the Highlands the most binding of all oaths was, or at least until lately, 'By the Black Stone of Iona', though in Iona itself it would probably be 'The Cross of St Martin'. The Black Stone is the eternal, immemorial Lia Fail which came to Scotland from Ireland. It is the Druidic Stone of Destiny; on it Colum crowned Aidan King of Argyll, it was taken after that to Dunstaffnage where the Lords of the Isles were crowned upon it, and then to Scone where the last of the Keltic Kings of Scotland was crowned. Now as the 'Coronation Stone' it rests in Westminster Abbey 'till Argyll be King'.

The Kelts' great Oath was by the falling of the sky. When they were fighting with Alexander the Great on the Ionian Sea they swore to him, 'If we observe not this engagement, may the sky fall on us and crush us, may the earth gape and swallow us up, may the sea burst out and overwhelm us.'

In the great Irish epic poem of the eighth century *Tain bo Cuailgne* – The Brown Bull of Quelgny – the Ulster heroes declare to their King, 'Heaven is above us and earth beneath us and the sea is round about us. Unless the sky shall fall with its showers of stars on the ground where we are camped, or unless the earth shall be rent by an earthquake, or unless the waves of the blue sea come over the forests of the living world, we shall not give ground.'

The Brown Bull is the Keltic counterpart of the Hindu Indra, the sky-god who is represented in Hindu myth as a mighty Bull, whose roaring is the thunder and who lets loose the rains 'like the cows streaming forth to pasture'; and the legend of the Brown Bull is the old story of the war between the sun and the night, each of whom desires the Bull of the Sky to be his property.

So old are our Mysteries that even the word Eden is of Keltic derivation, for it means Y Dinor, the Mound. The sacred word of the Druid priesthood was the Mound, symbolizing the earth with the trench round it as the immortal sea, whence it had been drawn up. The beehive shape of each tumulus or mound symbolized the Garden of the Lord. Each circle or mound was called T. Gwyn or Holy T. because on its summit stood the symbolic tree with the three golden apples, the tree which was made of an upright and a crossbar. At one time the whole Island of Britain was called Insula Pomorum, or Isle of Apples, and though subsequently this title was confined to Glastonbury, it shows how in the early days that set-apartness of our land was recognized. All through Britain may be greater and lesser mounds – the holier places in a holy land – and where there are traces of serpent worship and a mound, there will have been a seat of Druid culture and pre-Druid worship. Arthur's Seat in Edinburgh, the town of Eden in Westmorland, Cader Idris (Arthur's Chair) in Snowdonia, the Tor at Avalon, the old ruin on Great Orme's Head called Gogarth, which must surely be a corruption of God's Garth or Orchard – all these are holy places in this holy land.

Chapter 6

The horse and the Dragon

In the Keltic Mysteries in addition to the Great White Sow, which was the special attribute of Keridwen, there was one sacred animal which can actually be considered as two – the horse or dragon. For the dragon is really the winged horse, the flying horse which bears its rider to the throne of the gods. A careful distinction has to be drawn between the dragon of the kings and the great Worm or Serpent of Evil which is also called a dragon. In other words, there is the bad as well as the good dragon. Throughout Keltic literature there is continuous reference to the horse, to its supernatural powers and to its esoteric standing.

Throughout the centuries and throughout the western world the horse has been taken as the symbol of divine mind or reason. In Latin it is *equus*, which is a combination of Ek Hu, the great mind or spirit. According to Plato, when taken in the sense of its favourable meaning, the horse signified 'reason and opinion coursing about through natural things', and in its bad sense 'confusing fantasy'. Swedenborg points out that the significance of the horse as depicting the intellectual principle was shown by various ways in the Mysteries; 'but', he says, 'it is scarcely known to any here that the horse in a mystical sense signifies the understanding and that a fountain signifies truth; still less is it known that these significations were derived from the ancient church of the Gentiles.'

In all mythologies the horse figures as the steed of the sun god or goddess. He draws the car of light. In India, he is described as Surya 'who neighed as soon as he was born, emerging out of the waters' or as 'the Steed with Falcon's Wings and the Gazelle's

Feet', while the Dawn is said to lead forth 'the white and lovely
horse, Tig-Veda'. Surya the sun-god is also represented as being
drawn in a chariot over the skies by seven red mares – the Harits
or ruddy ones – his charioteer being Aruna. 'Seven mares bear
thee on, O far-seeing Surya, in they chariot, god of the flaming
locks. Surya has harnessed the seven Harits, daughters of the
car, self-yoked.' Since both Soma the moon and Agni the lightning
are but types or aspects of Surya, they also take the horse as
symbol.

The Royal Sacrifice in India is that of Aswamedha or Horse
Sacrifice described in the Rig-Samhita. On this occasion the
consecrated steed is addressed by the officiating priest as follows:
'May not the breath of life oppress thee when thou goest to the
gods; may not the axe injure thy bodies (the three forms of Sun,
Moon and Lightning), may not a hasty unskilled carver blundering
in his work cleave thy limbs wrongly. Forsooth thou diest not here,
nor dost thou suffer any injury; no, thou goest to the gods along
fair easy paths; the harits and the dappled deer will be thy
comrades.'

It is prescribed in the ritual of the Aswamedha that the horse
be slain by means of a knife of gold, because 'gold is light' and by
that means the sacrifice will go straight to the heavenly world – a
ritual direction which points to the solar origin of the ceremony.

Greek and Latin mythology attribute seven horses to the Chariot
of the Sun. Their names have been handed down as Bronte –
Thunder; Eos – Daybreak; Ethiops – Flashing; Ehton – Fiery;
Erytheios – Red-producer; Philogeia – Earth loving; Pyrois – Fiery,
and all of them are described as breathing fire from their nostrils.

The Scandinavian mythology, which is the nearest to our own,
has only two horses in the Chariot of the Sun – Arrakur, the Early
Waker and Alsvin, the Goer. These two precious steeds were
protected from the rays of the sun by great skins filled with air and
slung under their withers. So careful were the gods of these two
precious and powerful animals that they also devised the Shield
Svalin – the Cooler – and fixed it in front of the car to protect them
from the rays that might strike their backs. In this Scandinavian
version of the drive of the Sun God the guider of the chariot was
Sol, the Sun Maid, daughter of Mundifari the Giant and the wife of

Glaur or Glow. Dag, the Norse god of day also had his own chariot, but it was drawn by but a single steed called Skinfaxi or Shining Mane.

Aurora, goddess of Dawn, has also been called 'White-Horses' when she drove behind her pair, Lampos – Shining and Phaethon – Gleaming; but when her steed is Pegasus she is called Eos, or the One-Horsed.

The other daughter of the Scandinavian giant Mundifari was the Moon, Mani, whose car also had only one horse to draw it - Alsvider – the All-Swift. And indeed she needed a swift horse on her journeys, for she was ever pursued by the Wolves Skoll and Hati – Repulsion and Hatred – who tried to catch her up and devour her as she hurried across the sky, for with the destruction of Mani the world would be plunged into darkness. By day they chased Sol and by night Mani; there were terrible moments for those on earth watching the hunt when Sol or Mani was nearly caught; they knew of the danger for the sky grew dark with an eclipse.

Diana, as the moon goddess, was always equipped with white horses and to this day the Arabs call a white horse 'moon coloured'.

In the Vedic hymns the Ashvin or horsemen are invoked; they are the twin brothers of the Sun and the Dawn who drive in a chariot drawn by horses or by grey asses and are called 'dispellers of darkness'. They are kindly gods, healing the sick, giving sight to the blind, refreshing the weary Sun and generally benefiting mankind. They also protect physicians and preside over weddings.

The Norse Goddess of Death was Hel or Hela, who rode a three-legged horse when she left Niflheim. She comes on occasions to foretell disaster, sickness or plague on the world, or in an older version to collect the souls of the dead. Christianity laid its hand upon her in no light manner, for she was not originally the goddess of disaster but the goddess of merciful relief, who came to ease the weary bodies of their pain. But when the Christian Church came to make its readjustments, it conceived it necessary to send Hel back to Niflheim, and they did this so completely that they even caused converts to refer to the underworld of torment and darkness by her name. But the further back one traces her myth, the more beneficent Hel becomes. There is a legend that when Hermod the Swift wanted to visit her, he borrowed Odin's horse Sleipnir, but even then he had to travel the mystic nine days and nine nights before he reached the river Gioll, which forms the boundary of Niflheim as the Styx formed that of Hades. The bridge that crossed the river was made of glass as the symbol of the transition of plane, and though it hung by but a single hair all the dead had to pass over it. They usually crossed it in groups, accompanied by the waggons loaded with goods for use in the underworld and riding the horses slain at their funerals for the express purpose. But so light were they that they crossed safely in their hundreds. When Hermod rode over to bring back Baldur the Sun God the bridge shook under the hoofs of Sleipnir more than it did beneath the whole host of the dead.

Odin's wife, Frigga, had her own horse too, called Hofvarpnir, the Hoof-Thrower, but she did not ride upon it herself, reserving it for the use of her messenger Gna.

Manannan the Sea God had his horse called Splendid Mane, which he loaned to the Sun God Lugh. Splendid Mane had a magic bridle which is or was in the keeping of the Wilcox family. It has the property of safeguarding the family should any wish to work them evil by causing the reflection of the evildoer to appear in a pail of water specially drawn for the purpose.

While Manannan's steed and his individual name have come down to the present time, it is sad to find that Bran, God of the underworld, had his place usurped by St Michael of the White Steeds who became the Gaelic Neptune and god of both mountains and seas, but in Ireland the breakers are still called the White Horses of Manannan.

The creation of the horse is attributed to Vishnu in India; he infused a portion of his life-essence into the body of an immense tortoise in order to aid him in re-creating certain important things which had been lost in the Deluge, amongst which was the 'high-eared' horse, the supposed prototype of the breed. Generally speaking, the Indian myths refer to the horse as a fully developed self-conscious creature with powers of speech and as having existed long before the creation of man.

Indian mythology links the horse with the wind; Indra's companions in battle are the storm-winds or Maruts and their chariots are drawn by self-yoked dappled mares, fleet as birds. The Ulemas of Algeria also think that the wind is the parent of the horse. They say that when God wished to create the mare, He spoke to the wind, saying 'I will cause thee to bring forth a creature that shall bear all my worshippers, that shall be loved by my slaves and that will cause the despair of all who will not follow my laws.' Then, the mare having been created by the wind, God turned and spoke to her, saying 'I have made thee without an equal; the goods of this world shall be placed between thine eyes; everywhere I will make thee happy and preferred above all the beasts of the field, for tenderness shall be ever in the heart of thy master; good like for the chase and the retreat thou shalt fly, though wingless, and I will only place on thy back the men who know Me, who will offer Me prayers and thanksgivings; men who shall be my worshippers from one generation to another.'

The nearest approach to the centaur in the Western tradition is to be found in the early tales of the Irish mythology and in the story, oddly enough, of Tristram and Iseult. In the Irish myth there is a legendary animal called a 'morc', which had horse's ears and was supposed to have been one of the kings of the Fomors. A mythical king called Labraid Lonsech was also reputed to have horse's ears. In the oldest version of the Tristram story, Mark of Cornwall was probably a centaur. Marc or March means a horse and Marach is a rider. It was told of him, too, that he had horse's ears and he seems to have been a Keltic form of Midas. In both Gaelic and British tradition he is a king of the underworld and the first Tristram story is the ancient tale of Orpheus and Eurydice when Iseult as Spring is snatched from the hold of the dark winter king.

Since Odin when mounted rode grey Sleipnir, the Saxon banner of the White Horse was dedicated to him and venerated accordingly. The Wooden or Hooded Horse of Odin, the one-eyed god, is called in Wales Pale Mary or Mari Llwyd. It has been suggested that it is an attempt to Christianize an old rite but there is also a tradition of a very early princess who flourished in Gwent and is to be seen to this day mounted on her steed on a rock in Rhymney Dingle. The Feast of Odin was held round Christmas time at the winter solstice when horses were sacrificed to him, and since the Hooded Horse is blinded there is an obvious connection with the One-Eyed.

The Asa gods built for themselves their magnificent city in the heavens, Asgard, their fortress. Set high above the clouds, they surrounded it with beauty and the glory of shining light, upon a holy hill in the midst of a broad dark river. The sources of that river were the thunder vapours that rose from the roaring cauldron called 'the mother of waters'. Round Asgard there was a great wall, black as night, and but one entry therein, and that was called Odin's gate, the gate by which the dead passed through.

And within the city was the great Court of judgement where sat the twelve gods to whom Father Odin had given the power to rule. Like the forty-two assessors of the Egyptian Hall of judgement, the twelve Gods of the Northmen passed judgement on the souls.

The Wonder Tree that formed the centre of Asgard, round which the thunder clouds formed, was Yggdrasil, the great Ash, the tree which nourished and sustained all spiritual and physical life. It was the Holy Tree of the Northland as the Oak was of Britain. Its roots were said to suck up the waters of three eternal fountains, and the waters of these three springs mixed together gave eternal life.

The topmost branch of Yggdrasil was called Lerad, the peacemaker, and upon it sat a great eagle, while the never withering leaves of the tree formed the food of Odin's Divine Goat, Heidrun, who supplied the drink of the gods.

The mysteries of the Northern cult and of Odin, the Wise All-Father, the One-Eyed, were intended to teach men how to cross the bridge known as Bifrost, built of air and water; which led, as has been said, over the abyss. Baldur, the sun god, is the progenitor of all the initiates of the Northern rites; his death was the subject of the mysteries, as indeed the deaths of all the sun gods have been re-enacted in almost every country and every pantheon, and when the ceremonies were ended and the neophyte had been permitted to partake of the unveiled mysteries of Odin he was greeted in Baldur's name as one who had been born again though he had not yet passed through the gates of physical death.

The Wild Huntsman is a feature of all Western Tradition and teaching. The Wild Hunt was called in this country both Cain's Hunt and Herod's Hunt. The former name was no doubt given to it because, as will be shown later, the Welsh draw their descent from Gomer son of Japhet and they would have brought the old tales of their ancestors with them. Herod's Hunt is obviously a later innovation brought in by the Church, possibly to counteract the other idea, while the Hounds of Hel, now usually spelt Hell, need no explanation. To the majority the Wild Huntsman was in the north none other than Odin himself in his double aspect as god of the wind and god of the dead. He was to be heard specially in the wintertime and between Christmas and Twelfth Night, riding upon Sleipnir, whose eight feet were faster than the gale, and on whose teeth Odin, their inventor, first cut the runes. The oldest riddle to be found in the north runs 'Who are the Two that ride to the Thing? Three eyes have they together, ten feet and one tail, and thus they travel through the land.' Thing in the Northern speech stands for a meeting of people and not in the sense we use it to define an indefinite object. Lest Sleipnir should be hungry during the winter, and especially during his rides, the peasants usually left the last sheaf of corn standing in the fields for his eating.

In Mecklenburg it is the goddess who leads the hunt on a white horse – Frau Gode or Wode – who is the opposite of Odin and a form of the triple goddess. Unlike Odin, who rides to collect the dead, she goes on an errand of happiness and beneficence. In a German version of a later date, it is Dietrich of Bern who leads the Hunt and on other occasions it is Uller, the Winter God of the Northern mythology who is substituted for Odin. It was this substitution that led to the rather old canonization of Uller as St Hubert or probably originally St Ullert, who has to this day remained the patron saint of huntsmen. Gwyn ap Nudd, the Fairy King of the Welsh rides a black horse with round hooves and it is not difficult to see how he later became changed into the ghostly Herne the Hunter of Windsor Forest.

The abstention from eating horse-flesh which is practised by all Anglo-Saxons, whereas the Latin races think nothing of it, is probably due to a deeply ingrained taboo in the first place, because it would have been unthinkable to consume the sacred animal.

Probably this taboo was held to very strongly by the early converts to Christianity, for in 730 we find that Pope Gregory wrote to St Boniface, 'Thou hast permitted to some the flesh of the wild horse and to most that of the tame. Henceforward, holy brother, thou shalt in no wise allow it.' It is improbable that so definite a command would have been issued by the head of a Church which had overthrown the taboos of Judaism unless there had been some very strong reason behind it. The Church was anxious to win the so-called heathen to the cult of the new Dispensation and to encourage or even permit them to eat of the sacred animal was perhaps not the best way to go about it.

In 1722 took place the last execution of a witch in Scotland; she was accused of having turned her daughter into a pony and of then having got the devil to shoe her. What the daughter's evidence at her mother's trial was, has not come to light.

One of the very old incantations which has survived and has been Christianized ran originally as follows:

Baldur rade,
The foal slade.
He lighted and he righted.
Set joint to joint, bone to bone,
Sinew to sinew,
Heal in Odin's name.

Altered to 'The Lord rade, Heal in the Lord's name' this charm has survived if not to the present day at least till quite recent years. It must be chanted by the witch or warlock under the breath so that the bystanders do not hear. The late J. E. Brodie-Innes, in the *Occult Review* for May 1917, tells of meeting a Cornish driver who had had a poisoned thumb cured by a wise woman by the recital of this charm, the application of a special salve and a black thread with seven knots in it tied around the poisoned member.

But since each good thing has its appointed opposite or counterpart which in early times was naturally considered to be evil or dangerous, the two being practically synonymous, so the horse has its nightmare, which was a form of the Triple Goddess in her ancient or hag aspect. In *King Lear* we find 'He met the nightmare and her ninefold', which is a clear indication that the reference is intended for Hecate and the nine muses in attendance on the goddess. The nightmare stands for fascination or witchcraft – for that which is terrifying or untrue – and in that aspect Hecate was herself called simply Mare, which is basically the same word as mirage or false water.

Mare was a goddess form very much feared by the primitive people of the west and horse-brasses were originally intended to be amulets against her power. The most powerful of these were the designs embodying the Greek cross within a circle, representing the sun, thus giving the horses the benefit of the best of both worlds since the Cross would protect the Christianized and the Sun the others. A stone with a hole in it which was hung over the door of the stable or tied to the key was called a hag, halig or holy stone, as it was intended to keep out the hag who entered to torment the horses.

In his *Vulgar Errors* Sir Thomas Browne says, 'what natural effects can reasonably be expected when to prevent the Ephialtes or nightmare we hang a hollow stone in our stables?' Ephialtes means literally 'One who leaps upon' and indicates the tormenting desire of the night-hag to ride the horses. Gross actually goes so far as to say that a stone with a hole in it hung at the head of the bed will prevent nightmares and therefore it is called a hag stone. All naturally perforated flints could be used as hag stones.

Rowan trees being infallible against witch-craft, farmers used to have their whip handles made of this wood so that they could not be held up by attacks on their horses from the ever alert hag. These were called rowan-tree gads and were much esteemed. More especially in Yorkshire, if a cart became bogged or otherwise handicapped, if the carter had no rowan-tree gad he would make his way to the nearest tree where he could cut one with which to belabour the horse and drag the cart free.

With the cult of the horse comes naturally the cult of the horseshoe which has always been a subject of so-called superstition in the west. The horseshoe is really the presentation of the horned headdress of Isis and therefore it should always be nailed up with the horns uppermost. It is also a symbol of the young crescent moon, the spring loving aspect of the triple goddess, and in the Bible, and more especially in the Old Testament, it is translated as 'the horns of the altar'. The reason for this is that if the priest stands facing the altar he has the gospel horn or side upon his left hand and the epistle horn or side upon his right, and thus balanced with himself as the centre between them he can stand with confidence before the seat of the Almighty. Qabalistically, he is representing the middle pillar between the pillars of Justice and Mercy. To 'grasp the horns of the altar' therefore would be to take into oneself the astral projections from these two points or pillars and unite them in the centre pillar which is the direct pillar of union of man with God.

There are two other aspects of the horse to which reference should be made before going to the most famous horse of all in our own tradition – the White Horse of Shrivenham. These are the water horse and the corn horse. The water horse seems to be a purely Keltic tradition and to occur in no other mythology, though it may have a correspondence with the hippopotamus god of the Nile. It is chiefly found in the Scottish legends and is always a terrifying sight with tremendous teeth and immensely long wild hair, while it seizes its victims and carries them away to the underworld in its mouth, plunging beneath the whirlpool where it usually dwells.

By some process of translation which it is difficult to follow the water horse becomes the hobby horse. It is possible that there has been a correspondence between the water horse and the maypole through the mirror and the wand of the magician – by way of the mirror and the wand. Or it may have been in the nature of a phallic symbol, more especially when combined with the maypole, and draw the correspondence from the stallion, like the Indian horse Mamoiji. The hobby horse was an integral part of the ceremonies held on feast days, especially in the West of England where Lyonesse had once been known, and it is possible also that it had some loose connection with this, either as a memory of the drowning of the land or as the relic of a thanksgiving ceremony that humanity had been spared. But as a water horse in that part of England it probably had some connection with the birth of Nature when the sun drew the land into fertility from the depths of the water. The word 'hobby' is probably derived from an old English word 'hoby' which means a nag, or a small pet riding horse, which accounts for the common phrase of 'riding a hobby to death'.

The other individual and important horse in the Western Mystery Tradition is the Corn Horse, who is sacrificed for the fertility of the fields. The cult of the fertility gods is too well known to need elaboration here but it is interesting to note one or two special attributes in this part of the hemisphere. At Lille in Northern France the Corn Horse is said to live in the fields in the form of a horse invisible to man, and if a harvester appears to be overtired his companions say 'He has the fatigue of the horse'. In Scotland the last sheaf in the field should be left for the horse or the mare to eat, but if the thresher is too mean or too careless to do so, he is said to be 'beating the horse'. Near Betty in Wales, the harvesters call their midday sleep 'seeing the horse', and if the signal to break off work is not given at the right time by their leader, they will all start to neigh and declare that they will go at once to see the horse.

On the other side of the world in Assam the Garos celebrate the harvesting of the rice with a horse made of plantain and bamboo and placed in the house of the village headman. All night long they sing and dance round it and when morning comes they take it to the nearest river and set it afloat that it may go downstream and be lost till the next year comes round.

The most famous White Horse of England is the Shrivenham Horse in Berkshire. Though called a horse it is much more like a dragon in its anatomy and it seems obvious that it was intended to be taken as the Dragon-Horse and not as a steed to be mounted by men. Its design is full of symbolism. The mouth consists of the Two Rays of the Eternal Twins, the pairs of opposites, the male and female principles without which nothing can be brought into being, while the Head and Eye combined form the Circle with the Point within it, the symbol throughout the ages of Eternity.

The White Horse was the seat of a Mystery School of great antiquity – so great that no one has been able to assess its period with confident accuracy. That most English of all the English poets, G. K. Chesterton immortalized it in his *Ballad of the White Horse* and says of it simply:

> Before the Gods that made the Gods
> Had seen their sunrise pass

The White Horse of the White Horse Vale
Was cut out of the grass.

The teaching in this Mystery School took place literally upon the horse, the initiates being grouped along the body, the neophytes at the tail and the more senior members of the brotherhood towards the head. The priest instructor sat at the nostril and gave his teaching from there, so instituting the familiar saying 'straight from the horse's mouth' as something which must be indisputable.

There are other Horses in England but though some have symbolic significance there is none equal to that of Shrivenham, which is one of the most precious relics of our Western Tradition. There is a White Horse at Bratton but it is a genuine horse and is shown as a stallion with a crescent moon on its tail. This cannot be dedicated to Keridwen, because Keridwen herself is always the white mare, but the bard Taliesin speaks of 'the strong horse of the Crescent,' by which is usually understood a son of Keridwen by Nevion or Neptune, so that the Bratton Horse may well be a representation of the son of the Mother Goddess. On the other hand, the Saxons, in contradistinction to the Kelts, considered the moon to be masculine and it is possible that the Bratton Hill Horse was cut to commemorate a victory of Alfred over the Danes after the battle of 878; for, though Alfred himself might have become a Christian, most of his followers were far from forsaking the religion of their fathers.

Now comes the matter of the Dragons and how they fit into the teaching of the Western Mysteries. They have to be clearly differentiated, for when the Church took over the old religion, Dragons were lumped into one category and that an evil one. But the original Dragon is really the Flying Horse, Pegasus, the power rushing up to God. Moreover, he was also the Serpent or Worm of Wisdom, as at Great Orme's Head and the other holy places.

The old serpent dragon that Michael threw down from Heaven is allegoric of the change from one form of faith to another. The churches of St. Michael were deliberately built upon the high places of the old faith to keep down the wisdom of the past, which the priests chose to designate as evil. But all through the ages the Dragon has been a symbol of pride and glory to the West.

There is still a Welsh Dragon on the national flag of Wales, a perpetual reminder of the teaching of our mysteries and the triumph of the wisdom which we have inherited. There were Dragons rampant on the banners of the early Kings of Wessex and they were a part of the Tudor Arms. Arthur himself fought under the banner of the blood-red dragon from whom he claimed his sonship until he changed at Glastonbury and adopted a personal standard.

When the Dragon or Worm – as it is more frequently called in Scotland and the North of England – is 'loathly' it is evil – a symbol of power put to the wrong use. St George slays the Dragon and rescues the Maiden, and the Dragon there stands for the old wisdom which had to be changed as the process of evolution grew. It was necessary for the new life to flow more abundantly that men might proceed a little further along their slow path toward union with the Divine, and since the great transmuters are birth and death, the death of the old forms of worship had to take place, with all the attendant unhappiness and misunderstanding and pain that inevitably accompany these periods. The 'loathly worm' is the symbol of false knowledge, knowledge deliberately turned to evil purposes, and of a past stage in understanding. The old bonds must be loosened when the new age is inaugurated. We, standing at the start of the Aquarian Age, can see for ourselves how things are changing; the age of reason is with us so that our pictures of the combating of evil are not so simple and dramatic as dragon fighting in the physical or even the astral world, for our awareness of the latter is not so clear, ordinarily speaking, as it was to our forebears. We are faced with the most difficult task of fighting spiritual wickedness in high places; our work at the present time in the face of the materialistic and selfish outlook of the world is to keep alive the spirit of the Mysteries which we have inherited, to lose no awareness of their significance, but to relate them to the problems which this incarnation has called on us to solve.

Chapter 7

The Druids(1)

The great St Bernard of Chartres once wrote: 'We are like dwarfs who have climbed on to the shoulders of giants so that we may see more than they and further; not because of the sharpness of our own eyesight or the tallness of our stature, but because we have been lifted up and exalted by the greatness of the giants.' And this lifting up should give us also the power and the aptitude to look back as well as forward so that we may assess with some clarity and measure of accuracy that from which we have sprung. It is not merely a question of seeing where we are going; since history repeats itself with unfailing regularity it is essential that we should know also whence we have come and what has fashioned us into the kind of people and nation that we are today.

The greatest and the most enduring priesthood of the Western Mysteries was that of the Druids or Wise Men. They came to development by natural degrees but in their heyday they were among the great Schools of the World. So important was their part in forming and defining our tradition that it is necessary to consider them in considerable detail. Speaking generally, but little justice has been done to the Druids and their work. Like every other institution, the priesthood rose gradually to its zenith and then began to decline, decaying as the new dispensation came into its own, and pursued at last by the bitter hatred of the new Church, ever intolerant of its predecessor until the last dreadful day of massacre. They were persecuted too by the Romans, who saw in them the hereditary guardians of the Keltic individuality but though they retreated into their mountain fastnesses during the reign of Nero they were still unconquered.

Unfortunately, during the last century or so the general attitude towards them has been the kindly condescension and tolerance shown to the witch doctors of backward nations or peoples, with a touch of shame, perhaps, that we ourselves should so few centuries ago have been sunk in such childish or puerile errors. The Druids have been presented as a set of idolatrous priests spending their time in white nightgowns cutting down mistletoe with golden sickles for no known purpose and occasionally destroying their battle captives by burning them in wicker cages.

Crudities and cruelties no doubt there were, especially in the latter days, but the true story of the Druid priesthood is one of great wisdom, of profound knowledge and the highest integrity. They were the priests and teachers of the Mystery Schools of the West, which included Gaul as well as these islands. But so great was the standing of the priesthood in Britain that the Druids of Gaul were accustomed to come over here to study the teaching in its greatest purity. Julius Caesar commented, 'those who study it deeply, usually go to the islands and study there for a time.'

Schrader in his work *Reallexikon* says that the Keltic Druids were quite different from any other priesthoods of Western Europe and that it has never been known from where their origin sprang; we, with our perhaps great inner knowledge, are content to take it that their wisdom came with the basis of our mysteries from the great Temples of Atlantis.

There is an Irish tradition that the Druids set foot in Ireland about 700 years before St Patrick, that is about 270 BC though naturally the mysteries were being worked there long before that date. But again we must remember that time in matters of the spirit still may move very slowly and that in those early developing days it moved more slowly still, both outwardly and inwardly, and the Druid priesthood in all its grandeur was something which no doubt took centuries to develop and come to fruition. Connor is said to have been King of Ireland at the time of the Crucifixion and there is a legend that the Grail was originally a Druidic vase used only in the most solemn mysteries. The Druids of Britain are said to have been warned clairvoyantly of the Passion, as we know they saw the details of the Crucifixion, and so they sent over to Jerusalem their most sacred object to be used as the Cup and

Joseph of Arimathea subsequently brought it back. True or not – and probably we shall never know – it is a beautiful thought that the two dispensations should be so closely linked on all planes, even to the material one.

Even the Early Fathers accepted the Druid priesthood as being something outstanding, for Origen writes that the Druids were held up by the Roman philosophers as examples of wisdom and models for imitation on account of their pre-eminent merit, while Clement of Alexandria called Druidism 'a religion of philosophers' and likened it to that of the primitive Persians. He also maintained that they owed nothing to Pythagoras – as had been stated by others – but, on the contrary, claimed that Pythagoras visited the Druids in Gaul to be instructed in their theology and mysteries.

Pliny considered them to be the Magi of Gaul and others have held with us that they were of Atlantean descent. Nearer to our own time, Alexandre Bertrand maintains that there is a parallel to Druidism in the lamaseries of Tibet and Tartary, and there is certainly considerable resemblance between some of the Druid beliefs and symbols and those of the Brahmans. They had of course in common the attribute of every Mystery School of standing that silence must be preserved regarding the mysteries; they shared the veneration of serpents and they also equally regarded it as unlawful to eat ducks, hens or other winged flesh. Both Druids and Brahmans carried a staff or consecrated wand; that of the Brahmans was usually surmounted by a wheel or circle while the Druids regarded the circle with deep reverence as being the symbol of eternity. Curiously enough, each priesthood venerated white horses and worked in vast pyramidical heaps of stones. For the most part, the Brahman temples were in India as open to the sky as the Druid temples and groves in Britain.

The Druids had a firm and unshaken belief in both reincarnation and in the transmigration of souls; generally speaking they were men of the highest personal integrity and held sacred the knowledge of the mysteries. One of the difficulties in finding out much about their beliefs and their teaching is that they wrote down nothing except a few allegorical poems, the key to which was known only to the initiates, and they were always extremely reticent as to their articles of faith. There was one exception to this, their belief in immortality, which was so vivid that it coloured their daily words and actions. They claimed, and perhaps certainly with some justice, especially in those days, that to write something down was to destroy the talent of memory. Even in regard to the mundane laws of their stronghold the Isle of Man; many of them were never committed to writing but were taught by word of mouth alone and known by the term of 'Breast Laws'.

As with all esoteric schools, there was a centre, a stronghold of magical teaching, set upon a hill and difficult of access. The symbolic meaning of this is too obvious to need comment, but it is possible that in some cases this stronghold may be found on the plane of matter. Whether the Druid city actually existed as such it is pretty well impossible to determine; it was fully located, however, whether factually or only in the imagination. Davies refers to it as 'upon the road from the promontory of Lleyn to that part of the coast which is opposite Mona' (Anglesey); in his work on Camden, Gibson identifies it with the ruins of a very strong fortification encompassed by a triple wall on an eminence called Broich y Dinas – the Ridge of the Fortress or City, part of the summit of Penmaen. Within each wall of this city there remain the foundations of at least a hundred towers of about six yards in diameter, while the defences themselves were six feet in thickness. Whether or not this material locating was accurate cannot be proved.

The City itself was called Emrys, or the Ambrosial City, a name with a profoundly esoteric meaning; in the *Black Book of Caermarthen* and other early MSS it is spoken of as Dinas Affaraon – the City of the Higher Powers, and is referred to as being the centre of the mystical rites. Artists have always portrayed it as being walled and towered and set upon the top of inaccessible crags – peculiarities which belong to other Mystery Schools.

Emrys was also said to be the headquarters of the Pheryllt, the group of Druidic alchemists, who, according to an old chronicle, are supposed to have had a College at Oxford before the University was founded.

During that period of the evolution of the Mysteries when the great solar deity was known as Bel in the time of Prydain, son of Aedd the Great (the Arch-Druid), it is said that the dragons or horses which pulled the chariot of Keridwen were stabled in Emrys.

The early British mysteries are loosely defined but they were

generally grouped into Triads after the manner of the ancient Welsh
Bards. We are told by the Bards that there are three things to be
found everywhere – God, Truth and the Circle of Gwynvedd or
Knowledge – and that to know them is to be united with them; and
there are also three things which cannot be known – the plane of
the existence of God Alone, the length of Eternity and the Love of
God. In these two triads the basis of the Druid teaching appears
to be epitomized and to be one of high thought and all-embracing.

The Druids were the Lords of Time and Space; they looked
out into the vast expanses of the heavens and they saw the ordered
grouping of the planets and the changing places of the stars as the
seasons passed. They reverenced the sun, for they saw it as the
motivating power, the great creative light and heat, whether in
control of the seasons or in its life-giving propensities. They went
so far as to consider it an act of impiety ever to turn one's back
upon it – a point of etiquette which has survived to the present day
in the necessity of always facing royalty.

In ancient Wales, houses had to be built facing the sun, or at
least facing south and east; any old house which has been built
with its front facing north or west is to this day called Ty With, or
'House facing the wrong way'. In Welsh the word for house is Ty
because the Tau is the representation of the Keltic cross which
stood on the roof of each dwelling. The south is still called the Dor
or Right Hand Side, the north Gogledd or Sword Side and the west
Gorllewin or Great Side, the region of the reflection of light. When
they were about to consecrate an oak tree the Druids bound a
cross beam upon it if the natural branches were not sufficiently
prominent for their purpose. On the right branch they cut the
word Hesus; on the left, Belenus; and on the middle or upright of
the cross the word Taranis (not too far removed from Tammuz),
while above the cross beam on the tree they cut out Tau. It must
be remembered also that the sacred symbolic tree of the Druids,
such as the tree said to be growing in the Garden of the Hesperides,
was made from the upright and the cross beam, the golden apples
being pendant.

The Druids are said to have possessed no fewer than thirty-
one seats of learning in Britain, each of these being ranked as a
Cyfiath or City, the capital of a tribe. Some writers maintain that

there were as many as three Arch-Druids at one time, the office being one peculiar to this country and not found among the Druids of Gaul. Their seats were said to be at Caer Trois or London, Caer Erroc or York and Caer Leon in Monmouthshire – thus pretty well dividing the country. The last Arch-Druid is said to have been Bran the Blessed, contemporary with Joseph of Arimathea; it was thought that he was converted to Christianity and sent to Rome with Caractacus as a hostage. In old age he came back, still a Christian, and began to preach the gospel in South Wales opposite to Glastonbury; and as an old and venerable man he is said to have offered his own crystal or grail to the Abbey in token that it had prophesied the Incarnation of Jesus but was now no longer needed. The triple authority of the Arch-Druids may well have been a necessity at the height of the cult, for it has been estimated that at one time the students reached the enormous number of 60,000 at once.

That the Druids were held in the highest esteem by the rulers and thinkers of the great civilization of Rome is proved by the highly eulogistic terms in which they were spoken of and written about. It is after all the disinterested opinions of men standing outside the door of initiation but yet able to assess its value by the results it produces which can be taken as worthy of serious consideration. They had nothing to gain or lose by praising or denigrating the teachings of the Druids; they were capable of appreciating them dispassionately and lucidly.

Pomponius Mela writes of them: 'One of their dogmas has come to common knowledge, namely that souls are eternal and that there is another life in the infernal regions ... and it is for this reason that they burn or bury with their dead things appropriate to them in life, and that in times past they even used to defer the payment of debts till they had arrived in the other world.' With regard to this curiously practical piece of teaching, Valerius Maximus says of the Druids of Southern France: 'It is said that they lend to each other sums that are repayable in the next world, so firmly are they convinced that the souls of men are immortal.' Ammanus Marcellinus says: 'With grand contempt for mortal lot, the Druids professed the immortality of the soul.'

Mela also speaks of the Druids as 'teachers of wisdom' and as professing a knowledge of the size and shape of the world and the movements of the heavens and stars; he says they were the instructors of the Gallic nobles, as Caesar said they were of the Gallic Druids. Diviciacus, one of the Aeddan Druids, was a personal friend of Cicero, who said of him that he had 'that knowledge of nature which the Greeks call Physiologia'.

Julius Caesar wrote 'The Gauls state that they are all descended from a common father, Dis, and say that this is the true tradition of the Druids.' Dis was king of the underworld in the Greek pantheon which had penetrated to Southern France. As we know, in the Keltic pantheon he is Bran, who became St Brandan. His head was said to have been buried on the hill where the Tower of London now stands, and his instructions were 'Bury it in the White Mount, looking towards France, and no foreigner shall invade the land while it is there.' The curious story that Arthur dug it up is, one would think, an interpolation by some monk who wished to bolster up the Christianity of a later Arthur.

And we here contact the Grail story again, for Pwyll, the King of the Underworld of whom we have heard before, is symbolized by the crane, the one-legged bird which stands in the ooze. It is always the lame Fisher-King who holds the Grail when men may no longer gaze upon it. He is the ruler of the inner plane and it is to his castle that men must go when they seek for the blinding truth contained in the magic mirror and must learn to distinguish between illusion and truth.

What actually then was the formation of the Druid hierarchy? There was a long and severe training. Only freemen were admitted, as must obviously have been expected in the older traditions – was it not once said scornfully that the Christians permitted slaves to become full members of their church? – and the novitiate lasted twenty years. The initiation ceremonies included the bestowal of a tri-coloured robe of white, blue and green, emblematical of light, truth and hope. The tonsure was also worn and not only by Druids, for in Wales it was known as the badge of service in some kingly or noble households and was a mark of dignity giving respect to the wearer. It was different from the tonsure subsequently given to all priests of the Catholic Church; all hair in the front of the crown of the head was shaved and then the hair clipped short from ear to ear, the purpose in both cases of course being to free the powerful centre in the top of the head from any impediment. Druids habitually wore their hair short while laymen wore it long. Druids wore beards, indicative of their rank and leadership, somewhat as Pharaoh wore his official beard, though so far as one can find out the Druids' beards were natural growth and encouraged to grow long and loose, laymen being restricted to a moustache.

After the period of initiation was over, the Druids were divided into three classes – each wearing his own distinctive robe of white or green or blue. The priests wore the white robes, the Bards wore blue and the Ovates or Poets, called Ollaves in Ireland, wore green. Green and white were the royal national colours of the early British and it is due to this that the emblem of Wales is still the leek with its pale green leaves and white stalk – not to be confused in the modern trend of transmuting it into the daffodil or Lent lily. The leek is an honest, homely vegetable and it was chosen for the reason that its colouring matched that of the royal house. The young Princess Elizabeth, always emphasizing her father's Tudor origin, put her household into liveries of green and white before she came to the throne. And a bard has described a king at the head of his host: 'tall men followed him, a numberless host in green and white.'

As most people are aware, the great temples of Druid worship in the south were Avebury and Stonehenge. The vast stone circle of Avebury in the form of the serpent was called by the Druids Kyn Nyth (Kennet) and it symbolized the whole round flat-bottomed world surrounded by the sea. But Stonehenge was perhaps the mightiest and the best of the Druid Temples and is to-day probably the most visited. Dryden wrote of it:

> Where she, of all the Plaines of Britain that doth beare
> The name to be the first (renowned everiewhere)
> Hath worthily obtained that Stonehenge there should stand
> The first of Plaines, and that first wonder in the land.

While Stonehenge was the centre of the worship it must not be forgotten that it did not and does not stand alone. In the formation of a Gorsedd or Official Gathering of Bards it was essential to have a conventional circle of stones on the summit of some conspicuous rise; the stones had to be so placed that there was room for a man to stand between any two of them except at the easternmost point where the two stones most directly confronting the sunrise should have been sufficiently far apart to allow the passage of three men abreast and so form a gateway. Other smaller 'Stonehenges' are the Ring of Stenness in the Orkneys, and the Stone Circle in Callernish in Uig on the Isle of Lewis. In the Orkneys Circle there are two groups of stones, the smaller of which has fifteen stones about twelve feet high and a diameter of about a hundred feet, and nearby is a single large stone called the Stone of Odin.

There are of course other well-known stones throughout the countryside, some of which may be the remains of larger collections. In East Cumberland stand Long Meg and her Daughters, uprights of which Long Meg herself is twelve feet high and fourteen feet in circumference. The Rollright Stones or the King's Stones in Oxfordshire are probably connected with King Arthur, and near them is a cromlech called the Whispering Knights. Stanton Trew, several miles south of Bristol, has circles of stones said to be Arthurian memorials. All these remains probably point to Druid Temples and are among the oldest parts of our ancient heritage.

There were three presiding officers at a Druid Ceremony; he who sat in Cadeririath or the Chair of the Most High, the Principal in the East; Goronwy or the Moon in the West; and Fleidwr Flam, the officer representing the meridian sun in the south. The north, that strange place of silence and mystery, was never occupied; the trinity which ruled the ceremonies and the Great Unmanifest were together present. Assisting the three chief Druids were two other officers – Sywedyad or the Mystagogue who was at the side of the Arch-Druid, and Ys ywedydd, the Revealer of Secrets, or the Skryer, who read the inner meaning of the sights and sounds revealed to the officiating priests.

The very name of Kelt shows how strongly the religious aspect of their lives appealed to the Druids and their followers, for they considered themselves as a Chosen People and their name of Kelt is derived from Celu or Kelu, which means Children of the Most

High God. On Midsummer Day the following prayer was recited at Stonehenge and the other chief Druid centres in the land:

> God, our All-Father, permanent amid all change art Thou. Thou has ever been, and as Thou art, so shalt Thou ever be. We seek and find in Thee the glory of the Dawn. We seek and find Thee when the darkness of the Night has fled. The sleep of faith has ever led through Night to Dawn.

The Druids naturally considered that water was the first principle of all things and existed in an unsullied state of purity before the world was made; but its quality deteriorated when it was mixed with earth. The earth, however, was venerated by them as the mother of mankind and particular honour was paid to trees as symbols of the immense protective power of the earth. For many centuries the Druids refused to build roofed temples, or even walled ones, considering it an outrage that the Deity should be considered as being confined within any limits save the vault of the sky and the depth of the forest. The numerous references to the groves are therefore simply references to the actual temples of the Druids; temple building was a later development. The sanctity of Anglesey was largely due to its numerous groves of oak trees.

According to the Druid belief, the clouds were composed of the souls of men who were waiting for reincarnation, being unable to unite with the sun, the source of all purity and life, as they were not yet perfected. The souls who had advanced further beyond the necessity for earthly reincarnation were thought to inhabit vast iceplanes on the moon, where they lost all their perceptions save that of simple existence until the time came for their next step in progress. The sun itself, according to this lore, consisted of a group of pure souls 'floating on an ocean of bliss'. After being thrice purified in the sun, these souls passed on to even higher spheres, while a meteor was supposed to carry the soul of a Druid straight to Paradise. So deeply did the Druids believe in the spiritual nature of man that one of their axioms read 'God cannot be matter and what is not matter must be God'.

When Christianity came to Britain the beliefs of the Druids were so close to those of the new teaching that they had little or no difficulty in being 'converted'; they were baptized and accepted new traditions and definitions but fundamentally their faith was unchanged. St Augustine himself declared later that their philosophy almost approached that of Christian monotheism. No idol or graven image has been discovered among the Druid remains, although Caesar arrogantly declared 'the countries of the Druids were full of idols'. But the basic purity of the Druid faith is exemplified in the Triad: 'In every intelligence there is thought; in every thought there is good and evil; in every evil there is death; in every good there is life; in every life there is God.'

The Pelagian heresy was closely allied with the ancient doctrine and teaching of the Druids. For the Pelagians held that baptism was unnecessary in Christianity, since the font was the symbol of natural birth, and the spiritual birth was from the Navis or Womb, called in Greek the Ketos or Whale or Ketena – a boat – so that Pelagius held that no water should be or need be used in baptism.

In Druid cosmology it was taught that seven times seven equals the seven great cosmic periods with the seven lesser periods of which each one is made up. 'Seventy times seven' of the gospel teaching would therefore mean until the end of time. According to Pliny, the Britannic month began when the moon was six days old instead of at the new moon, as the Druids considered that when she had reached her first quarter her power was of sufficient force for the working of moon magic, and this should be done at the beginning of the month. Their official 'new moon' therefore was a moon of one quarter.

A work published in the 16th century and called *Helvetia Antiqua et Nova* claimed that the Britons had as their divinities Theutates or Taut – which is the same as Thoth, Hesus, who is believed to be the equivalent of an early Gaulish god called Aesir or Aes, Belinus, a sun god, and Cisa and Penninus who were probably gods respectively of valleys and hills.

Taut represents the universal father to whom was attributed the invention of writing, which the Druids used in the form of the Ogham script, devised by Ogmion, son of Dagda. The language embodied in the Ogham symbols was in fact Old Keltic, the forerunner of Gaelic. The Druids also used the system of tree-writing or Bobileth, called in Old Keltic Bethluison. This consisted of an alphabet of thirty-four characters each represented by a different tree and the script could be made up by the various leaves being strung on a cord, each representing a single letter. The same principle was adopted by the ancient Peruvian Indians when they sent quipas or messages by knotted strings, or by the wampum belts of the North American Indians. It is to this tree-writing that Taliesin alludes when he says in one song 'I know every reed or twig in the cavern of the chief designer.'

It was Edward Davies who first noticed that in all Keltic languages the initial letters of trees stand for letters of the alphabet. Beth-Luis-On stands for Birch, Rowan, Ash. So many of the Druid ceremonies were connected with twigs and trees in general that it is reasonable to find such a language, and also to find that the Beech-tree is a common symbol for literature; the reason for this is that writing tablets were usually made from beech wood which has a surface soft enough to take impressions.

Other than Keridwen the great mother, the god the most favoured and beloved was probably the sun god, Hu the Mighty, who, as we have seen, is also Taliesin the Wonder Child. He is also sometimes called Cadwalladar, but most usually Hu or Hu Gadarn, under which title he became the Keltic equivalent of Hercules. Iolo Goch, the 14th-century bard, describes him as 'Hu the Mighty, the Sovereign, the Head Protector, the King, the Giver of Wine and Renown, the Emperor of the Land and the Seas and the Life of all in the World, was he. After the Deluge he held the strong-beamed plough, active and excellent; this did our Lord, stimulating the genius that he might show to the proud man and to the humble wise the art which was most approved by the Ancient Father; nor is the sentiment false.'

Chapter 8

The Druids(2)

In their teaching the Druids emphasized both the active and the passive phases of life. They were fully cognisant of the importance of the pairs of opposites and their philosophy and mystery teaching were largely based on this fundamental.

They believed that every year at the vernal equinox the 'essence of life' was brought afresh from the source of all elements across the water. It was brought by the sacred boat or Ark, propelled by Keridwen. The Ark plays so large a part in the Druid ceremonies and rituals that a chapter will be given to it later in this book. For the moment, let us just remember that since the Essence was brought in this crescent-shaped boat it is not unnatural that it should frequently be assumed that the Cauldron of Keridwen was a moon-shaped vessel and not a circular pot. The physical or material form is not important; whether it were cauldron or boat or crystal mirror, it was still the source of life.

The Essence having been brought to this country regularly, it was equally regularly warmed by Gwion Bach, the Little White God, who is the God of Nature and may be considered here as the Pan of the Druids – the young Pan of the woods and fields, not the Pan of panic. And this brings us to a very important difference in the teaching of the Druids from that of other religions. In the Druid teaching there was insistence on Two Eggs of Life in the form of the consolidated Essence. And these two Eggs represented the bodies of the Sun and of the Earth, for the Druids held that the Sun also had a new body yearly, derived from a separate substance but of the same nature as the body of the Earth. This is the Second

Egg to which Pliny the Younger refers when he writes of the Druids holding such in veneration. In other mysteries there is but one Egg – the new life in embryo; but in the Western traditions there are two.

This is a mystery of very considerable importance. The first Egg represents the substance of earth if fertilized by the heat which comes from natural warmth; but the other Egg is fertilized by the Seminal Word, and the Word therefore becomes the Father of his own Sun's body. When this mystery is under consideration the Cauldron is usually referred to as the Nydd or Nest, as 'pointer' to the reference.

The pure Essence of creation came, the Druids believed, from Keridwen herself, the mother of all, Binah of the Tree of Life, she who forms matter from spirit, the eternal sea from whom all life is primarily drawn. But in the East it gradually came to be believed that the Sun was created annually in a cave from the body of a young goddess and that he was then transferred to the barge of the Great Mother who is Keridwen in the West and Isis in Egypt and Parvati in the East, and that while he was in the Boat or Shrine the Word of God was miraculously introduced into his head. It was in this manner that Bacchus was transferred from the virgin Semele to the Ark – which is the outward form of the Great Mother – Moses from Miriam into the ark of rushes on the Nile; Jesus born of Mary in the cave received the Word while in the Jordan; the Dove descending upon him is called his baptism, and it is this same dove which is represented as having annually descended on the head of the young Horus while he ascended from the crescent-shaped moon-barge of his mother Isis, or as the wren which the Western Mysteries say descended on the head of Taliesin as he stood up in his boat.

This birth from the boat is universally called regeneration. The original Egg was a goddess, Creirwy daughter of Keridwen, and before the adoption of the Egg as a symbol of life she was herself the representation of the Essence in the sacred barge – the first generation of the body of the Sun. This first generation was of the Earth and the second of Heaven – the advent of the Divine Word or Dove or Wren uniting herself with the earth of the Body of the Sun.

It is for these reasons that Keridwen is sometimes alluded to as a Hen, the parent of the essential Egg, sometimes as a Serpent and sometimes as a Fish, for the Egg is the symbol of life in all three kingdoms of animal life. The Greek word for Womb is Delphus, which is easily transmuted into Dolphin, so that the Dolphin is frequently substituted for the Barge or Ark of the new birth. In the Western Mysteries the great fish is used for the symbol of the boat – the Whale (which swallowed Jonah and set him forth regenerated) is called Ketus from Ked, the Protector or Preserver. And sometimes Keridwen herself is called the Navis or Boat, from which comes the Nave of the Church, in which sit those who have passed through the second birth at the font, which is the symbol of the virgin, Creirwy or Semele or Mary, standing at the foot of the Nave or Navis as it does in the East. In the West the Church has deliberately changed the significance of the old rite and has made the Font the symbol of the spiritual birthplace and the rite of Confirmation the spiritual rebirth.

The two Eggs having been warmed by Nature, Three Drops descended into the cauldron from Heaven, thereby transmitting the eternal life force. In the Western tradition it is stated that this was a great surprise to Keridwen, and this surprise has a symbolic interpretation, for it is intended quite simply to convey that there was no question of physical intercourse between the gods and that the life force was engendered by spiritual means. From these Three Drops rise three streams, corresponding to the three pillars of the Tree of Life – representing the male, the female and the united in equal expression of power. These Three Drops can also be described as Three Rays and are taken by some authorities to represent the beginning of all Art, the first Ray bringing down Vision, the second Symbols or Letters and the third Understanding – the union of the other two.

When the sacred Tree was set up it was made like the Calvary Cross and was not necessarily a real tree. The Equator was symbolized by the trunk and one arm pointed north and the other south, to indicate the glory of the sun and its beneficence to the earth on the one hand and the mystery of the dark north, whence came all hidden knowledge, on the other. The three Apples may still be seen above the doors of Jewish homes where they are

called Ayin or Eyes or Fountains – from which came vision and
the out-pouring of Wisdom.

But the most strongly defined characteristic or attribute of the
Three Drops is that they signify the Mark of Cain.

The Arrow which Abaris the Druid presented to Pythagoras
at the Olympic Games is the 'sacred sign'; it was put upon Cain
not for his condemnation but for his protection. It is the Broad
Arrow once commonly used as the mark of all Government
property – i.e. basically the mark of the King – the hieroglyph
denoting the Word, whose living emblems are the Dove in the
East and Wren in the West. Other variations are to be found in
the Fleur-de-Lys in France, the Trefoil or Shamrock, and the
Three Plumes of the Diadem of Wales. The Cymry claim their
descent from Gomer, son of Japhet, direct descendant of
Abraham, and when Cain went out 'into the wilderness' he went
to the Land of Nod, which is the Keltic word for a Sign. Nodi is
the Welsh verb for signing or giving assent and so we still find
the nod in all Britain used as the silent mark of agreement. Cain,
it must always be remembered, begat Enoch, the great teacher
and seer, and it was through Cain that the knowledge was passed
on. Abel must die because the period of his evolution has passed;
the mark of the new era is on Cain, who goes out as his successors
went into the wilderness or down into Egypt to become initiates
and to spread the Word.

A title of the Sun in Wales on 25 June is still Cyvrin or Cain, and
they refer to the Secret Mark of Nod Cyvrin, which means the
Sign within the Circle.

In Druid mythology the Day of the Cauldron is 21 December
by solar time – the day of the winter solstice – but by the Egyptian
and Roman calendar it is the 26th day of December. The four
great Festivals were May Day, Midsummer Day, 1 November and
10 March, which they called New Year's Day, for the Great Day
of the Cauldron was a sacred occasion and not a general feast.
The festival of May Day was instituted to commemorate the leaving
of the Ark by Hu Gadarn and his family, for Hu Gadarn is the
Keltic Noah. Since he was also the sun god it is called Beltaine
after his predecessor Beli and that is the name which has persisted
most to this day. At the May Day feast the Sun entered Taurus,

the bull being the sacred animal of Hu Gadarn. Oxen were placed near a lake in the centre of which was a holy isle and the shrine or ark was drawn from this through shallow water by means of a chain while the singers sang a chant called Cainic y Yehain Banawg, a melody said to represent the lowing of cattle and the rattle of chains. The principal Druid in the subsequent procession was said to represent the Arch-Druid with his wand of power, who was followed by no fewer than two hundred Druids and Bards, the latter carrying harps, while the Ark was then raised upon the shoulders of the Ovates and disciples. Immediately before it in the procession went the Hierophant, representing the Supreme Creator; then a torchbearer representing the Sun and then the Herald Bard who was the Moon.

The Druid harp was a harp of seven strings, emblems of the lines of the Seven Spheres of the Seven Planets, the voice of the Druid being the eighth note needed to complete the great Octave. The term 'Seven Spirits of God' is an old Druidic method of describing the Sun which passed through the seven planetary spheres during the year, transmitting seven times the Wisdom of the Emanations of the Creator down to Earth by the agency of the Sun as Seven Notes of Music or Harmony: In his opening chapters of the Apocalypse, St John writing to the seven churches in Asia uses the symbology of the Seven Notes of the Sphere.

Midsummer Day was the great Feast of the Sun in his glory; the fires were lighted on the hills and the earth was deemed to be at the height of its annual fecundity. Later on this feast was merged or adopted into the Church as the Feast of St John and this change seems to have been brought about without much difficulty.

1 November was of course Samhain, the great Feast of All Fairies, when the 'lambswool' was drunk and the Sidhe rode abroad.

10 March as New Year's Day was the occasion of comparatively mild celebration but it did mark the beginning of the spring and of the new year when the sun entered Aries, the first of the Zodiacal signs. In the dark three months there was no celebration, nor feasting nor rejoicing; the early seeds had not shown themselves; the earth was germinating and there was darkness over the land.

The Druids taught the manifestation of God through His

Creations and they 'worshipped' Him in nature, but they did not regard the individual elements as essentially divine in themselves. The real foundation of their belief was that each element, each corporeal body, was the seat or temple of a subordinate deity who resided there and directed its operations – the active principle of the passive form. They held that whatever came to pass in Nature from the rustling of leaves to the mightiest storm or flood was the carrying out in Nature of the laws of God – that Nature was moved by the divine laws unhelped or unhindered by human agency; so they gave particular attention to natural but unusual appearances and actions such as falling thunderbolts or woodland fires, to the flight of birds and their songs at unusual times or seasons – in fact to all that was not instinctive in the animal races. With this attention to the unexpected in Nature they classed also the *involuntary* actions of men, claiming that these were the manifestations of the intentions of God, indications of forthcoming events, instructions or warnings that should be considered and heeded.

Their belief was in one sovereign God with diverse lesser deities working under His instructions and subordinate to Him. Their sanctuaries were given the names of the gods who presided over them and the Druids maintained that the Supreme Being had created a number of intelligences which animated the different spheres of nature and matter in general and assisted people to reach the destined end planned for them by the Eternal Will. They regarded these Intelligences as Angels or Spirits but considered them to be capable of acting only in accordance with and under the guidance of the Supreme, who instructed them in his Will. He, the Supreme, was represented by the Sun, but the Sun as the sun was not worshipped; it was the great symbol of the Living God known as Aesus or Hesus or Supreme Light, self-existent and invisible, yet seeing, penetrating and knowing all things – in three words, Omnipresent, Omnipotent and Omniscient. Contrary to the practice of the Greeks and the Romans, the Kelts did not elevate their heroes to the dignity of gods but kept them merely as mortals superior to the general run of mankind.

Since the Druids worshipped the Supreme Being in the guise of the Sun, most of their rituals began and ended with a procession going thrice round the temple or grove or altar in the course of the

Sun. Until recently in the Scottish Highlands women with child used to go three times round a chapel for easy delivery, while sick persons went three times round a cairn. In Melrose the old Masonic Lodge either elected its new office bearers or installed its new Master on the Eve of St John, when the brethren walked in procession three times round the market cross. After dinner they went out again, two and two abreast, each carrying a lighted torch. Preceded by their banners, they again made a triple tour of the market cross and then a triple circuit of the Abbey. According to an old Highland belief, as soon as a child is born – or as soon as possible – and best at noontide and facing the sun – the mother should take it and touch its brow to the earth in sign of recognition. This is known as 'The Old Mothering' and acknowledges the source of life in the earth animated by the sun.

A good deal has been said in various books on the subject of the 'Serpents' Eggs' of the Druids. Some people have considered these to be prehistoric beads of blue or green glass, called Snakestone in Cornwall, Wales and Scotland, and Druids' glass in Ireland. But the Druids would have been familiar with these and would not have considered them natural objects with magical value. Nor, as will be seen in a moment, do they correspond with Pliny's description. It is possible that they were ammonites, but as the Druids were known to the Welsh Bards as Naddred or Adders (regeneration – by the sloughing of the old skin) they were in all probability glass balls covered with skin. They were or could have been used as amulets; they were thought to be lucky in legislation as signifying a just ending to a case.

Pliny wrote of them: 'There is also another kind of egg in much renown in the Gallic provinces but ignored by the Greeks. In the summer numberless snakes entwine themselves into a ball, held together by a secretion from their bodies and by their spittle. This is called anguinum. The Druids say that hissing serpents throw this up into the air and that it must be caught in a cloak and not allowed to touch the ground, and that one must instantly take to flight on horseback as the serpents will pursue until some stream cuts them off. It may be tested, they say, by seeing if it floats against the current of a river, even though it be set in gold. But as it is the way of magicians to cast a cunning veil about their frauds, they pretend these eggs can only be taken on a certain day of the moon, as though it rested with mankind to make the moon and the serpents accord as to the moment of operation. I myself, however, have seen one of these eggs; it was round and about as large as a smallish apple; the shell was cartilaginous and pocked like the arms of a polypus. The Druids esteem it highly. It is said to ensure success in lawsuits and a favourable reception with princes, but this is false, because a man of the Vocontii, who was also a Roman knight, kept one of these eggs in his bosom during a trial and was put to death by the Emperor Claudius, as far as I can see, for that reason alone.'

We can discount much of Pliny's 'spleen' and his contempt for the Serpents' Eggs, but his description does bear out the idea of the skin covered beads. As for the Gentleman of the Vocontii who was also a Knight of Rome – we do not know if his cause was just! The Egg could hardly be expected to prevail against righteousness.

There were three great pillars of the Druid State; the first was Hu the Mighty, the second was Prydain, son of Aedd the Arch-Druid, who first organized social conditions and sovereignty in Britain, and the third was Dynvwall Moelmud, who first made a scheme for laws, maxims, customs and privileges for the country as a whole and for the tribes in particular.

When invoking, the Druid priest identified himself with the Supreme Being; he acknowledged only one God and his prayer was made direct to the Throne. One which has been preserved is as follows:

Am not I called Gorlasser the Eternal? My Best (?) has been a rainbow enveloping my foe. Am I not a protecting prince in darkness to him, who presents my form at both ends of the hive? Am I not a Plougher? Have I not protected my sanctuary and with the aid of my friends caused the wrathful ones to vanish? Have I not shed the blood of the indignant in bold warfare against the sons of the Giant Nur? Have I not imparted of my guardian power a ninth portion in the prowess of Arthur? Did I not give to Henen the tremendous sword of the enchanter? Did not I perform the rites of purification when Hearndor moved with toil to the top of the hill? I was subjected to the yoke for my affliction; but commensurate was my confidence; the world had no existence were it not for my progeny? Privileged on the covered mount, O Hu with the expanded wings, has been thy son, thy bardic proclaimer, they deputy, O father Deon; my voice has recited the death song where the mound representing the world is constructed of stonework. Let the countenance of Prydain, let the Glancing Hu attend to me.

The birds of wrath securely went to Mona to demand a sudden shower of the sorceress; but the goddess of the silver wheel of auspicious mien, the dawn of serenity, the greatest restrainer of sadness, on behalf of the Britons, speedily threw round his hall the stream of the rainbow; a stream which scares away violence from the earth, and causes the vane of its former state round the circle of the world to subside. The books of the ruler of the mount record no falsehood. The chair of the preserver remains here; and till the doom it shall continue in Europe.

It is a magnificent prose poem of immense power when chanted by a Druid priest of high rank – and none other would have been likely to take upon himself the great responsibility of identification for the purposes of magic with the Supreme Being in His own form.

Druid initiations were of considerable length and a great strain for the neophyte, who must have been not only impressed but even filled with genuine fear at some parts of the ritual. They required physical as well as mental and spiritual courage and they were conducted with immense pomp and solemnity.

In the Druid rituals one most important feature of the initiation ceremony was a drink compounded of herbs and known as the Brew of Keridwen. It was otherwise called the Stream of Gwyion and it was held that to drink it gave a man genius and inspiration. Composed of a mixture of herbs, mistletoe was added as a last ingredient.

It must be remembered that to the Druids mistletoe signified the essence of life. It was called in Welsh Pren purauer or Tree of pure gold, or Pren annwyn, Tree of the ether of space, or sometimes Pren uchelvar, Tree of the lofty summit or high place. According to Lewis Spence, mistletoe was so highly thought of that the bosses on the reproductions of Keridwen's cauldron should be considered as mistletoe berries, since the Cauldron held the essence of all life. Great ceremony was observed in the cutting thereof, which could only be done by an initiate or holy one, robed in white and with bare feet ritually washed in pure water, while the actual cutting was done with a knife of pure gold, representing the young sickle moon and the origin of our own harvest sickle.

The Kadeir Taliesin gives a list of the components of Keridwen's Brew. These are: flowers; perfect convolutions; primroses; vervain; points of trees of purpose; solution of doubts; mutual pledges; worldwide wine; deep water. These components are a mixture of symbolic materials and abstractions and must therefore be considered as having a deep interpretative meaning, since by themselves they do not make sense.

Flowers as a whole are intended as a symbol of the pure magic to be used in the initiation; perfect convolutions stand for the formulae of the rites which must be done without error and in due form; primroses in Welsh are called briallu, which is a word meaning 'dignity-capacity' – the essential for a practising Druid; they are always considered as being the flower of the fairies; vervain is the accepted symbol for soothsaying or foretelling the future. It is interesting to note that when the Druids picked vervain they did so at the rising of Sothis the Dog Star 'without being looked upon by either sun or moon'. In gathering it, the earth was first propitiated by a libation of honey and it had to be picked or dug up with the left hand – which is the active hand upon the plane of magic where all outward forms are reversed. Points of trees of purpose stand for Bethluison, the language of trees; solution of doubts means the oral training given to the neophyte; mutual pledges represent the sworn brotherhood of a fraternity; worldwide wine is the symbol everywhere of admission to fraternal friendship and hospitality, or to the feast of learning; deep water signifies the purifying rites or baptism of the candidate.

The Brew therefore consisted of certain material herbs and flowers impregnated with the thoughts and aspirations of the other abstract ingredients which vivified it and of which both the candidate and the officiating Druids were fully aware.

Then 'when the Brewer who presided over the cauldron of the five plants shall have given it a boiling' the mistletoe was added, to be boiled last, and the draught was then given to the candidate. This corresponded with the time when he had completed the period of his strenuous training, and the first part of the initiation was conferred in the magic brew. He was now ready for the exhausting practical ceremonial.

After the drinking of the sacred Brew came the Initiation of the First Death. This was a symbolic rendering of the time when Noah was enclosed in the Ark. The candidate was placed for a period of time in a cave or in a hole made in the side of a ship and there left alone to meditate in solitary darkness and to combat the powers of evil which assailed him. He was in due time released from this confinement at a moment in the ritual known as his Second Birth and he then endured the ordeal of the Second Death. To accomplish this he was placed in a coracle with a top covering it. This represented the Ark on the Eve of May before it had been drawn from the waters of the lake on the Feast of Hu Gadarn. The coracle was then launched on the tidal water of a river which symbolized the Deluge. Swept down on the stream, the candidate in darkness, tossed and turned upon the flowing river, the coracle was finally brought to rest by the stranding of it on land left dry by the ebbing tide, at a spot called the Mount of Debarkation or Regeneration or the Stone of Ascent which was the scene of the Third Birth.

After the disembarkation and as part of the Ceremony of the Third Birth the candidate shared for the first time in the Hidden Wine of the Esoteric Circle of the Druids and became a fully initiated member. Taliesin says 'Bright wine is the beverage of the narrow circle'. The initiate was now called Derwydd or Blessed or Recovered, and the spot on which he had landed from the coracle was known to him afterwards as the Spot of the Supreme Proprietor.

The most probable setting for this tremendous initiation ceremony would have been Bardsey Island, which had always been a sacred place since the disappearance there of the first Merlin and where the ebb and flow of the tide and the exposure of the Stone of Ascent would be possible under certain conditions. It can easily be seen what a great similarity there is in these initiation ceremonies to those of Ancient Egypt or to the Eastern traditions. The sequestration of the candidate alone and in the silent darkness is common to all, as is the symbolic Rebirth. In all religions there is to be found sooner or later the sacramental meal whether it be bread and wine or water or salt; the essential symbolism is the communion of the brotherhood.

Chapter 9

The Ark and the Wren

It may perhaps come as a surprise to those who are not yet conversant with the traditions of the Western mysteries to know that the Ark plays a very large part in them – not so much the Ark of the Covenant as the actual Ark of the Deluge.

All through the Western teaching comes this story of the Ark. It is the Ship of Destiny, the very core of the symbology of the teaching. As will be seen in another chapter, the Cymry or Kelts or Chosen People claimed descent from the tribes living round Mount Baris or Ararat, and it is from this early date that they draw the teachings of the mystery of the Ark.

Comparisons with teachings of other forms of worship show how important was the Sacred Boat in whatever form it may have been pictured, and how the saving of man from destruction was a fundamental theme throughout the known world. We may therefore safely assume that the evolution, so to speak, of the Deluge and the Ark which saved the chosen few was the result of a great new period of initiation in the evolution of the world. Before the recorded day of the Ark, we are told in Genesis that 'God saw the wickedness of man was great in the earth and that every imagination of the thoughts of his heart was evil continually'. And we have already learned from an earlier chapter of Genesis that there were men called Giants who were the offspring of the Sons of God and the daughters of men. It is probably also reasonable to assume that these pre-Deluge men misused their powers and that the Deluge was sent to wipe them out and to inaugurate the new cycle. It does not matter very much if the Deluge be in Atlantis or in the centre of Asia – the principle of the thing is the same – the destruction by a vast catastrophe of evil which has grown out of hand. When it is remembered that the marginal reference in the Authorized Version to the quotation given above notes that for 'every imagination' one may substitute 'the whole imagination' and that the Hebrew wording signifies not only the imagination but 'the purposes and desires' it would be hard to suppose a state of greater positive wickedness.

The text of the Bible is quite clear in the differentiation of the elect and the corrupt. 'And the Lord said I will destroy man whom I have created from the face of the ground; both man and beast and creeping thing and fowl of the air; for it repenteth me that I have made them; But Noah found grace in the eyes of the Lord.'

The text of the Qabalah interprets this as follows: 'And Tetragrammation said: I will destroy Adam who I have created from off the face of Ha-Adamah, the earth.'

The Ark or boat or ship is always represented as the saviour of the world because it esoterically represents the navis or womb in which the seed of the new generation is carried for safety. And so through all the mystery teachings we find the boat is pre-eminent in the story of transition from one stage of evolution to another. The story of the Argo and the Heroes who set out to find the Golden Fleece is one of the fairy tales of the Middle West – a fairy tale that may have come with the Cimmerii from Ararat and been deposited on the way with its basis of the Deluge and the few saved who went out to seek the ways of God. It is the story of all the heroes who set sail to find the Wisdom of the Spirit, the fleece of the golden ram when Aries rules the skies. In the Norse version of the story the boat is the Vessel of the Einheirar or Heroes, carrying them across the dark waters to Valhalla; it is Charon's boat over the Styx in another sense, for it takes the dead to the kingdom of their Tir n'an Oige.

Procopius (500-565) tells in his book *De Bello Gallico* that all Britain is divided by a wall. He talks of the barrenness of the north and refers to it as being inhabited by vipers and other dangerous reptiles and 'the natives affirm that if any one passing the wall (which was the mountain range of Snowdonia) should proceed to the other side, he would die immediately'. And he adds, significantly, 'They say that the souls of men departed are always conducted to this place.'

The Breton legend of the boats of the dead is one that can make even a balanced person shiver. Thirteen fishermen from the Breton coast are regularly compelled to ferry over at dead of night the souls of all those dead who die in Brittany. These shades are unseen by the rowers but are assembled and marshalled by a mysterious ghostly leader. Those fishermen who are selected to row the dead must go to bed early for at midnight they will be roused by a tapping at the door and the voice of some one calling to them softly but imperatively. They rise and go down to the shore, compelled by some strange force which they cannot identify and cannot resist. Here they find their boats riding at anchor and to all appearances empty, yet low in the water as if filled to the bulwarks. Getting in themselves, they settle to their oars and pull steadily in silence. In normal times the passage between Brittany and the coast of Britain takes a day and a half, yet on these occasions it is usually completed within an hour. When the boats are beached on the opposite shore, the fishermen rest on their oars. Still they see nothing, but as the dead rise and file on land the boats ride ever higher in the water. Then from the shore a loud voice is heard calling the roll of the dead by name and style, and so they go to their last home in the lands of shadow.

So deeply is this tradition engraved on the minds of the Bretons that at Reguier it is still the custom to convey the dead to the churchyard by boat over a part of the river called 'Passage de l'Enfer' instead of taking the shorter road by land to the grave.

In reading of these ancient customs it should be remembered that Arvor or Armor is the usual name for Brittany. The name actually means the Sea-Washed Land, as in the district called Morbihan or Little Sea. Arvor is the poetic name of a part of Basse Bretagne only. In the Gaelic Brittany is called Brealunn-Beag – Little Britain – and in Welsh it is Llydaw.

On All Souls' Eve the Kelts of Brittany still spread a feast for the hungry dead, even as the Egyptians used to do. In Ireland the feast of All Souls is known as La Sambha, derived from Sambh or Repose from Labour. Saman is one of the names of Buddha, regarded by the ancient Irish as the lord of the dead. And it is worth noticing that one of the great days is the day of All Souls' Eve, called Samhain or All Fairies, since it was to the Sidhe that the souls of the dead were conducted. There is a legend that the people of the Sidhe are themselves the dead, waiting to be reborn, spending the intervening years in a dim paradise under the earth. But since to partake of the food of the dead is to know of no return from their country, those who visit there must neither eat nor drink, no matter how pressing the invitation. It is the world wide story of Thomas of Ercildoune, who spent seven years among the Sidhe but was warned by the Fairy Queen to eat neither apples nor pears lest he should never return to his own folk.

Death and the life thereafter play an enormous part in all the Keltic traditions, as indeed they must do in the mysteries of a people supremely conscious of the transitory nature of this world and firmly convinced of the joys of the heavenly one.

Our present Michaelmas ceremonies are derived from the so-called pagan creed of our own past. In the Hebrides there is a song called the Iollach Michael or the Triumph Song of Michael. He is as St Michael the patron saint of the shore and of the folk who dwell upon it; not always was he the warrior saint, the shining Archangel who flung Lucifer from heaven. He is the St George of the sea coasts, the guardian angel of all fishermen and sailors. Deeper still and further back in our traditions, he is a mixture of Neptune and Poseidon; before that he was in all probability Bel, the ancient Keltic god whose cattle are the waves, and behind Bel he is Manannan, the God of all Waters, whose boat was called Ocean Sweeper, revealed to us as the father of an Immortal Clan.

There is a story that the night Columba died Michael came over the seas on a flood of light which was made from a cloud of angelic wings and that he sang to the saint a song which none but Colum heard, ere he gave his soul into the hands of Michael to be carried up to God. This is a Christian legend but it may well have its original counterpart in the old old story of how Manannan came to Cuchullin in the land of the Sidhe. For the stories are the same; it is only the embroidery and the nomenclature of the personnel that change, as the old men die and the young men tell the stories again and the hero of yesterday becomes the god of the day before.

For all those who worshipped at Mount Baris and revered the Ark it had a deeper significance than to those who did not understand the basis of the worship – for the Kelts it was the

Baris, Ark or Ship of the Queen of Heaven, which became later known in Greece as the Delphos or Womb. It was the birthplace of the new God, the son of Keridwen the Mother Goddess. The symbol of the Ark in the west is usually the logan stone or rocking stone – the stone of the incarnate word, for Logan and Logos are very near basically to one another. In Wales these are called Maer Sigl or Shaking Stones. In some cases the top of the great rocking stone is hollow and has within its depression another small stone, typifying even more clearly its symbolic significance. In so easy a manner did the womb of the mother become the Cauldron of Keridwen, giving birth to all life. The swaying rocking stone was a clear symbol of the swaying boat of the Queen of Heaven as she sailed through the sky in her vessel resembling the crescent moon.

The Sacred Boat of the Druids is the Thebet of the Egyptians. It is immaterial whether it be the bearer of Keridwen or of Isis, for both are the eternal mother goddess, both bringing the new born babe who is the herald of the new age.

Sometimes the Ark or Boat of Keridwen is shown with two disks at the prow and stern; in this aspect Keridwen bears the title of Gwrach, the Warrior Goddess, and the boat is called Dinas or the Fortress and it is intended to symbolize the protection given to the infant god. Gwrach means actually the Woman with the Heart of a Man and from it we get our word Virago, debased now but originally the symbol of the protecting mother, the bird turning on the robber of the nest, the lioness springing to defend her young.

In the tradition of Greece, Gwrach is paralleled with Pallas Athene, for Pallas means the Shield. And this leads us to the fascinating question of the Palladium or Shield of the country. In Greece, Argo claimed that it held the Palladium, as indeed it did, for the Argo is the Sacred Ship, which we find still commemorated in the nave of the Christian Church where the roof is often ribbed, while the Nave or Navis is the body of the building from which springs all life. According to the mysteries of the Kabiri, that strange sect which survived on the islands of the Mediterranean and about whose rites but little is known, the Greeks made a cardinal and far-reaching mistake when they handed down their esoteric teaching, for they confused Hipha, a galley or ship with Hippa, a mare. Thus they misrepresented the Sun as a horse with a colt, the son of the Sun and the Mother Goddess, and called him Pegasus. But it was a misunderstanding and a mistake in oral teaching which had very far-reaching consequences for from it arose all the story of the Trojan War and the Wooden Horse of Troy, which was no horse but a ship concealing armed men. Even so late a writer as Virgil says of it 'Its sides are planked with pines', which would make it a very curious horse but a very reasonable ship.

The Palladium or Shield of England is declared to be Stonehenge. Here the great British Ark is represented as moored under the earth, the columnar supports being symbolized by three enormous upright stones which once stood like the three legs of an upturned British stool. Lying upon their summit was the vast Cromlech (Crome-ach or Big Stone). Beneath them lay hidden the sacred ark from which the Divine Essence was concealed and prepared for emission. And this is the explanation of the Druid ceremony of Midsummer Day; it was to symbolize the moment when the sun struck upon the concealed Ark and fertilized the life within it.

The spread of the worship of the Ark can be seen by the images of it which can still be seen for instance in the Arms of Dunwich in East Anglia or the Arms of Portsmouth, which show a star rising above a rocking stone.

The Druids believed that the Ark travelled regularly between this world and the next, extending its journey beneath the earth until it rose once more out of the east. In Wales, a coffin is still called an ark in the vernacular and it is laden with flowers to symbolize the land of the Blessed to which it conveys the immortal soul. At Druid funerals the usual decoration was the white waterlily, a flower which must have been brought from the east, for though it is found in numerous places both in Wales and England it is not indigenous. The white water-lily is kin to the lotus of the East and the nenuphar or sacred lily of Egypt, and it was chosen as the sacred plant, partly on account of its long strong stem, which symbolized the umbilical cord of Hu Gadarn, son of Keridwen.

One might term Noah's Ark the first Ark; the second Ark the Ark of Moses in the bull-rushes, for Moses is also the representative of Horus the young Sun god; he is drawn up out of the water by Pharaoh's daughter, after being placed there by Miriam, the eternal mother, whose name is only the Hebrew of Mary – which in turn is Marah, Bitter – the Bitter Sea of the first feminine principle in the Sephiroth of the Tree of Life.

One of the papyri in the British Museum states in allusion to the boat of Isis conveying the young Horus: 'The Boat of the Rising Sun hath a fair wind and the heart of him that is in its Shrine rejoiceth. O thou mighty youth, thou Everlasting Son, self-begotten, who didst give birth to thyself.'

In the Mystery teaching of the West as in all other mystery teachings there is the symbolic story of the Babe drawn up out of the water. In the Keltic tradition it is Hu Gadarn under his other name of Taliesin – a name that has its confusion for the reader because it is applied not only to the young God but to the Bards on many occasions and is a generic rather than a specialized name. Keridwen planned the destruction of her son Taliesin to whom it will be remembered she gave birth after first swallowing him in his earlier form of Gwyion; but because he was so beautiful she could not bring herself to kill him but finally placed him in a leather bag and threw him into the river. The bag, being made of leather, has special significance for it gives some indications of the period of the story since it was during the Taurean epoch and the bull worship then prevalent among the bards. The Bull-hide was the sacred hide used by the priests. The bag containing the child did not sink but was carried downstream by the current until it was brought up against the poles of a weir on one of which it caught and hung. Here King Elphin, who represents the wise ruler, had come to fish for salmon. Salmon being the symbol of the heavenly wisdom it is not unnatural that it should be the king who draws up the Child who brings the new knowledge with him.

The whole story of Taliesin can be found in the song cycle called by that name. It is believed to cover the initiation and the quest of the initiate for wisdom through the ascending stages of the power of vision.

A Druidical hymn of the Deluge has survived to the present time and is an interesting document illustrating the quality of the literary invocation. The gaps in the translation are those left by the translator.

The inundation will surround us, the chief priests of Ked. Yet complete is my Chair in Caer Sidi. Neither disorder nor age will suppress him that is within it. It is known to Manawya and Pryderi that three loud strains round the fire will be sung before it whilst the currents of the sea are round its borders and the copious fountain is open from above, the liquor within it is sweeter than delicious wine.

O thou proprietor of heaven and earth to whom great wisdom is attributed, a holy sanctuary there is on the surface of the ocean. May its chief be joyful in the splendid festival and at the same time when the sea rises with expanding energy. Frequently does the surge assail the Bards over their vessels of mead; and on the day when the billows come from beyond the green spot, from the region of the Picts. A holy sanctuary is there on the wide lake, a city not protected with walls; the sea surrounds it. Demandest thou O Britain to whom this can be mostly applied? Before the lake of the son of Erbin let thy ox be stationed. A holy sanctuary there is upon the ninth wave. Holy are its inhabitants in preserving themselves. They will not associate in the bonds of Pollution. A holy sanctuary there is; it is rendered complete by the rehearsal, the hymn and the birds of the mountain. Smooth are its lays in its periodical festival; and my lord duly observant of the splendid mover before he entered his earthly cell in the border of the circle, gave me mead and wine out of the deep crystal cup.

A holy sanctuary there is within the gulf; there every one is kindly presented with his portion. A holy sanctuary there is with its productions of the vessels of Ked. The writings of Prydain are the first objects of anxious regard; should the waves disturb their foundations I would, if necessary, again conceal them deep in the cell. A holy sanctuary there is upon the margin of the flood; there shall every one be kindly presented with his wishes.

Disturbed is the land in praise of Hu, the island of the severe remunerator; even Mona of the generous bowls which animate vigour, the island whose barrier is the Mena, Deplorable is the fate of Aeddon (Adonis) since it is perceived that there neither ... the ark of... has been or will be his equal in the hour of perturbation. When Aeddon came from the land of Gwydion into Seon of the strong door a pure poison diffused itself for four successive nights whilst the season was as yet severe. His contemporaries fell. The woods afforded them no shelter when the wind rose in their skirts. Then Math and Eunydd, masters of the magic wand, set the elements at large; but in the living Gwydion and Amaetheon there was a resource of counsel to impress the front of his shield with the prevalent form, a form irresistable. Thus the mighty combination of his chosen ranks was not overwhelmed by the sea. Disturbed is the island of the Praise of Hu, the island of the severe inspector (Noah). Before Buddwas may the community of the Cymry remain in tranquillity; he being the dragon chief, the proprietor, the rightful claimant in Britain. What shall consume a ruler of the illustrious circle? The four damsels having ended their lamentation have performed their last offices. But the just ones toiled; on the sea which had no land long did they dwell; of their integrity it was that they did not endure the extremity of distress.

As has been intimated earlier, the sacred bird of the Western mysteries was not the Dove but the Wren. The wren is the smallest of all Western birds and when it builds a nest it builds it in the form of a ball and then conceals itself therein. This is the symbolic rendering of the manner in which the Word of God conceals itself in the human heart. When the Druids were in the habit of burning the bodies of their dead on funeral pyres they enclosed a wren within each ark or coffin, symbolizing the continued existence of the soul freed from the body. Though not a similar ceremony it has some affiliation with the rising of the Phoenix from the ashes.

In the old days the word 'hen' was the old British word for bird, generically speaking, and was not confined to the farmyard fowl or else differentiated from the cock bird. Keridwen as Henwen, as she is called in the cycle when she is pursuing Gwyion is the White Bird and though the story says that she turned herself into a hen, this is a particularized bird not meant in the original version. The White Bird is more likely to have been a White Swan when it is remembered that this is the emblem of Bride the young goddess.

The old Lowland Scots rhyme ran:

> Malisons, malisons, mair than ten
> That harry the Lady of Heaven's hen.

And the Lady of Heaven here is Keridwen, and her 'hen' is her son Taliesin in the form of the wren or Word of God.

Later on, when the true tradition of the wren had been forgotten,
it became the custom to go 'wren-hunting' at New Year. Originally
this had been a joyful but solemn ceremony when each man went
out by himself to hunt for the hidden wisdom and he who found the
actual wren believed that he had been blessed with the inner
knowledge of God for the ensuing year. But it became in the end
merely a cruel sport in which young men and boys went out to
catch the wren and exhibit it at the village doors for a small tip for
'luck'. This habit of 'wrenning' took place in France, Ireland,
Wales, the Lowlands of Scotland and parts of England, and
wherever it was found, it may be taken that a large Druid settlement
was formerly in the locality.

Sir James Frazer points out the similarity between the cult of
the snake tribes of the Punjab and the worshippers of the wren.
In most European countries the wren is designated the king of the
birds – the hedge king, the little king, and to slay one was thought
extremely unlucky. If any one harries a wren or spoils its nest he
will meet with disaster before the year is out. At St Donan, in
Brittany, it is thought that if children tamper with a wren's nest
they will suffer from pimples on face and legs.

The wren was officially hunted on various days in the winter
months, and it must be remembered that this was not for cruelty or
for sport but for solemn ritual reasons – again it is the old belief
that the death of the god gives his strength to the killer and renders
the latter semi-divine. It is a natural development of the fertility
rites and the killing of the old king to pass his kingly power to his
successor. Mistletoe, being the prime phallic emblem, the formal
cutting of it by the Druids was emblematic of the emasculation of
the old king and the descent of power to his junior.

In the Isle of Man, that stronghold of Druid worship, the wren
was hunted on Christmas Eve, or rather in the early hours of
Christmas morning, down to the eighteenth century. After the
midnight bell on Christmas Eve the servants of the house, none of
whom had gone to bed, went out to hunt the wren. They
subsequently killed it and fastened the body to a long pole, the
wings extended in the form of the God with outstretched wings,
and carried it in procession round the village, stopping at every
house while the old song was sung:

We hunted the wren for Robin the Bobbin,
We hunted the wren for Jack of the Can,
We hunted the wren for Robin the Bobbin,
We hunted the wren for every one.

Mr Lewis Spense points out that this rhyme probably alludes to the old sun god Beli, whom he co-relates with Robin the Bobbin, and with the Will o' the Wisp or 'Kit of the Canstick'. This is quite possible; both are deities of light – one of the morning and one of the evening, and the wren, the light of the spirit representing the sun at mid-day would make the third of the Trinity.

The Manx ritual continues with the burying of the wren 'with the utmost solemnity, singing dirges'. These were called 'the wren's knell' and only when they were over did Christmas proper begin. It is easy to see how Druidism was translated into Christianity and the death of the old King made to fit in with the birth of Christ.

About the middle of the nineteenth century the Feast of the Wren was transferred to St Stephen's Day, 26 December, in the Isle of Man. In Pembrokeshire a wren known as 'The King' used to be carried round on Twelfth Day in a box with glass windows surmounted by a wheel, the spokes of which were decorated with many coloured ribbons; the men and boys who carried this from house to house sang songs of goodwill and cheer. It is possible that the glass windowed box was a far-off representation of the glass house into which Merlin retired, and the presence of the wren within it indicated the original holiness of the symbol. In the South of France from Carcassonne to Marseille variations of the old custom took place, usually on New Year's Eve.

In the Isle of Man there is a variation of the Taliesin origin of the wren-hunting. There is a story that once there lived a fairy-girl or mermaid who lured youths into the sea; one of them cast a spear at her and to avoid it she turned herself into a wren but had to assume her own shape on every New Year's Day. On that day she was at the mercy of the humans, who chased and hunted her, and killed her if possible, in order to avenge their friends whom she had lured to destruction. Each feather from such a wren was supposed to preserve a sailor from harm and no Manxman would willingly put to sea without one.

The Druids considered the wren not only as the sacred bird of Taliesin but as an oracle; they drew inferences from its chirping, believing it to tell the will of the gods; the Irish Glossary of Cormac calls it the Drui-en or Druid bird.

From the West Highlands of Scotland originates the legend that the wren was called King of the Birds because it sat upon the back of the Eagle, which had claimed the title of flying higher than any other bird; when it had reached its limit of strength the wren flew above it crying 'Behold your King' – a legend that can be easily traced back to Taliesin, the sun god in the British Pantheon.

Chapter 10

St John the Kelt

The first suggestion of the idea that St John the Divine was a Kelt came from a paper given in the Scottish Lodge of the Theosophical Society in 1894. The paper was read to the members and on the next occasion it was commented upon by the Chairman, who added some most useful hints.

What grounds are there for this fascinating theory? First of all, remembering that the Cimmerii or the original Kelts came from the mountains round Ararat and Persia and migrated westward through Greece and Egypt, it is reasonable to suppose that there was at least a residuum which remained *en route*, so to speak. A great migration does not mean the picking up of an entire people and the placing of it intact in another place; there must always be those who do not complete the journey but bring their history and culture to the lands through which the chief migration passes. Moreover a migration of this size takes many years to accomplish and before it has reached its goal even another generation has taken charge. If the evidence is good enough to support the proposition there is no reasonable or practicable ground to refuse it.

What is the chief characteristic of the Kelt – more especially of the Welshman? The true Kelt is the mystic 'seeking a sign'. Basically a commingling of the Brythonic, Goidel and pre-Aryan races, he may well have brought with him to Cymry some of the dark mystery and magic of those ancient peoples. He is ever the seeker. Consider the Welsh Captain in Shakespeare's *Richard II*, in Act II, Scene 4:

> 'Tis thought the King is dead; we will not stay
> The baytrees in our country are all withered
> And Meteors fright the fixed stars of heaven;
> The pale faced moon looks bloody on the earth
> And lean look'd prophets whisper fearful change;
> Rich men look sad and ruffians dance and leap,
> The one in fear to lose what they enjoy,
> The other to enjoy by rage and war:
> These signs forerun the death or fall of kings.

Shakespeare knew his Welsh mind, and here is the captain talking to no less a person than Lord Salisbury of omens and signs and taking it for granted that these foretell the death of the King of which he knows nothing planned.

The Welshman speaks, writes and thinks in symbols and interprets prophecies and facts in his own peculiarly symbolic and mystical manner. His interpretations and allusions therefore are always much more involved than those of the non-Kelt.

The usual theory is that the ancient mysteries were carried from Egypt to Greece, to Asia Minor and to the shores of Thrace and penetrated to these islands, presumably by seafarers, who found the Hibernian schools well settled in and the Atlantean teaching established as the foundation. Setting Atlantis aside, let us examine this theory for a moment. It falls to pieces on consideration. In every one of the old world kingdoms there is a religion which is more or less pure, more or less corrupt, based on a common form, whether it be Moloch and Tanith in Carthage, or Dagon and Atergatis on the Syrian coasts, the great mother Diana of Ephesus, the supreme fertility goddess, Set and Osiris in Egypt. And across this worship there springs a light, a gleam of something pure and mystic, some glimpse of mysteries that really were divine, which grows by virtue of the truth concealed in it. Such mysteries were to be found in old Atlantis but not in the ancient pantheons which succeeded the pure worship in the story of these islands. The germ was there but the expression of the higher truth had become lost. This was inevitable as the new era was ushered in; the intuitive wisdom had been lost as men grew to think with their minds and, in so doing, they descended further into matter and the new awakening had to be brought to their consciousness.

This gleam, this tiny star is found in every country which reflects the Keltic element, and this is of major importance, because it is the one thing which binds together all these different religions; the common truth, however differently it may be expressed. And if we look to see at what stage in the evolution of a religion this element appears, which substituted the common ideas and symbolism of a great and universal truth for the warring of the lesser tribal gods, it can be found that its first appearance synchronizes in each case with some great Keltic migration; and so the Kelts, tumultuous and warlike, creating commotion in every country through which they passed and in which some of them remained, yet brought with them and left behind the foundation of the universal brotherhood in the teaching of a common faith in One Supreme Ineffable – God Omnipotent, Omnipresent and Omniscient – the Lord and Ruler of all the pantheons.

We know that the Kelts themselves thought they were the Children of the One Great God – Celu – the Chosen People – and it was this belief in the Supreme Being which characterized their religion and their whole outlook.

History records that about forty years after the death of Alexander the Great in 278 BC there was a great incursion of Kelts into Asia Minor where they were defeated in battle by Antiochus I, son of Seleucus who founded the Seleucid Dynasty in Asia Minor. Seleucus was himself the son of Antiochus, one of Alexander's generals, and was granted his overlordship after the successful campaigns. For delivering them from the peril of the Kelts Antiochus was called Sotor or Saviour by his subjects, but curiously enough the appellation in reverse had an appropriate meaning. He is said to have placed a ring fence round the province finally inhabited by the Kelts in order to protect others from their inroads but by so doing he actually preserved the Keltic integrity for they were thus unable to mix with the other tribes of Asia minor and so preserved their religion, their characteristics and their character. So intact and untouched was their language that six hundred years later St Jerome reports that he found them speaking Gaelic and totally indifferent to the common tongue which was used round them.

The province in which they settled was called Galatia after

them, since they were indifferently known as Kelts or Gauls. A
reading of the third chapter of the Epistle of St Paul to the Galatians
gives an unusual number of references to Abraham to whom of
course the Kelts were closely allied in descent, since they traced
their ancestry to Japhet, whereas Abraham was the lineal
descendant of Shem.

Admonished by St Paul for backsliding, the Galatians are told
'Know ye, therefore, that they which are of faith, the same are
the children of Abraham ... So then they which be of the faith, are
blessed with faithful Abraham', references which made to a non-
Jewish people are a clear indication of their unity and solidarity as
a race.

Having so prepared the ground, what of St John? First let us
consider his personal appearance as he is shown traditionally in
the paintings throughout the early and mediaeval schools. We know
that such paintings are not portraits in the accepted sense of the
word; they are what might better be termed representations which
have grown up through the centuries as symbolic pictures of the
Holy Family and the Apostles. Some one must have been the
originator of these types and it is reasonable to suppose that they
were founded on oral tradition.

St Peter is always clearly recognizable; he is a big, brawny
man with fiery eyes and a dark, thick beard. He is full of muscular
energy that radiates from the canvas. He is symbolic of that
enthusiasm and strength with which he cried out that he would
follow the Lord and with the impatience which caused him to smite
off the servant's ear.

But look at the traditional pictures of St John. Here are
completely different attributes; the long, usually fair hair, the
beardless face, the nervous rather than the physical energy which
animates him – these are all the attributes of the Kelt as are the
clairvoyance and dreamy meditation which he displays in his writing.
The earliest crude drawings are in the Catacombs and from replicas
of these the two extremely different basic traits of the Apostles
can be seen, showing that it is a tradition which goes back to the
earliest Christian times.

If the Gospel and the Epistles of St John are read it will, I think,
be seen that they are far more flowing in their symbology, far
more allusive with indirect information than the other three Synoptic

Gospels and the Epistles of, say, St Paul and St Jude. St John has a poetry in his writing which will not be denied.

The opening of his Gospel is the natural opening of the Kelt who has come to Christianity. There is the basic Keltic certainty that in the beginning there was the Word – Logos – the Supreme Being – 'the same was in the beginning with God'. That is not Jewish in its approach. Those first five verses separate St John from the other Apostles.

The three other Evangelists, be it noted, always speak of 'the people', but St John invariably writes 'The Jews', as though they were to him foreigners. Ouspensky says: 'St John's Gospel is a quite exceptional literary work. It is written with tremendous emotional upheaval ... It cannot be understood by the mind at all. One feels in it an emotional excitement on the level of ecstasy.' And what of the Apocalypse? Here is the poetry and the imagery of the Kelt from the first word to the last – the whole of the great Vision lies before us in a glowing tapestry of Angels and Jewels and Riders upon Horses, and among them One sitting upon a Throne so superbly described in symbols that sometimes it is almost possible to catch a glimpse of the reality that lies behind them. Here again and upon the higher arc is the Land of Tir n'an Oige, no longer beneath the earth but glorious in the heavens. It is the Vision Glorious vouchsafed to the clairvoyant and translated as best he could – and who but he was better equipped to do so – into the mystic and mysterious symbols that came naturally to his mind.

If the Letter to the Seven Churches in Asia be read in Welsh it becomes not merely magnificent prose but full of poetry and continuous 'hwyl' – that untranslatable word for 'spirit' or 'essence' or the lordliness which is of another sphere. Read as a continuous poem, the Letter shows the characteristic note of the oldest Welsh poetry in that each section is terminated by a promise or proposition.

This triad form is the peculiar attribute of the Keltic period. In each triad the first two lines are so to speak make-weights, the purpose of the verse being in the third line, so that the sense of the whole is created by reading the third lines one after the other. The curious structure of the triad is accounted for by the rhythm required for it to be sung to the Welsh harp. If the Epistle to the Seven Churches be read in Welsh in its entirety as seven separate letters this characteristic is, I understand from a Welsh scholar, quite marked. If it is read in English the final admonition to each Church should be read consecutively and without the intervening verses so that the message may be found as it was actually intended to be given. This might be taken as corroborative 'internal' evidence that St John was a Kelt since no other race would have used such poetic and symbolic language.

There is further reasonable evidence in Chapter 21, verses 7-8. 'He that overcometh shall inherit all things ... But the fearful and unbelieving . . . shall have their part in the lake which burneth with fire and brimstone: which is the second death.'

These verses compare the position of those outside the Church with the Circle of Abred or transmigration.

Sharon Turner writes, concerning the Bardic script of Llewelyn Sion:

> The Bards mention three circles of existence. 1. The Cylch y Ceugant, or all-enclosing circle, which contains the Deity alone. 2. The Circle of Gwynvydd or Felicity, the abode of good men who have passed through their terrestrial changes. 3. The Circle of Abred or Evil in which mankind pass through their various stages of existence before they qualify to enter in the Circle of Felicity.
> All animated creatures have three stages of existence to pass through ... in passing through the changes of being attached to the state of Abred. It is possible for man by misconduct to fall back retrograde into the lowest state from which he had emerged.

The return to the second death in the Keltic religion meant a return to the circle of animals, as they held that men had become so by transmigration but that they could revert.

According to Sharon Turner Falsehood will plunge a man back into some degrading form, while Cruelty may condemn him to transmigration into a ferocious beast. Liars and murderers are specially mentioned by St John in his list of those who are to be condemned to the second death.

The hell of the eastern and southern nations is burning hot and it is from the teaching of the East that we get our notions of fire and brimstone. But the hell of the northern people is the cold white deadness of the icebound regions, where Hel reigned. According to the Druid teaching animals were clothed in fur or hair by protective Nature because they had to traverse the circles of Abred with its bitter cold in order to reach the Line of Liberty – that is of free will, above which men and women existed – unclad by Nature save in skin because they had free will and could choose where they would go and what they would do.

'Humanity was the limit of degrading transmigration; all the changes above humanity were felicitating and they were to be perpetual, with ever increasing acquisitions of knowledge and happiness.'

It is St John the Kelt, and no Jewish writer, who could say 'To him that overcometh will I give to eat of the tree of life which is in the midst of the paradise of God.'

Chapter 11

The history of our Race

A s was suggested in an earlier chapter, the headquarters of
the Cimmerii or Gomerii – the sons of Gomer, son of Japhet
– were in the earliest days around the Mount of Ararat.
Like other peoples, they spread west and south and they were to
be found later occupying the countries from the Danube to the
Caspian Sea. Like other people, they moved westward in one of
the big migrations of history and continued through the centuries
to move even further west till they came to the hills and valleys of
Wales. Here the Hibernian mystery schools were still flourishing
but the Cymry or Chosen People brought with them their own
traditions and their newer ritual of evolution which created a later
phase in the development of the Western Mystery Teaching.

It is not the purpose of this book to delve into the various
composition of the Kelts – Brythonic, Goidelic and so forth – but
to give just the outline of the story which belongs to us all.

According to Herodotus: 'the Kelts are outside the Pillars of
Hercules and they border on the Kynetae who dwell farther away
towards the west of the inhabitants of Europe.' Ancient writers
locate the Kynetes in the west of Spain, which, says Sir John Rhys,
'suggests a still more important inference – namely that there
existed in Herodotus' time a continental people of the same origin
and habits as the non-Keltic aborigines of these islands. The word
Kennet has been assigned to a Keltic root of unknown meaning,
but Herodotus speaks of a race called Kynetes or Kynesii.'

Rhys suggests that the Brythons were the Belgae and the
Goidels the Kelts – two of the three parts of Gaul; the third part
was represented by the Aquitanians, who have no correspondence

with the other two races. The Goidels probably came to Britain first, being pushed westward and across the Channel by the Brythoni or Belgae. When the Kelts arrived they pushed the Iberians into the hills and caves and even out of the country, just as the Iberians had previously superseded the Milesians. At the time of the Roman occupation the Brythons held pretty well all the land of England south of the Tweed except for the extreme West, while the Goidels or Kelts occupied the Cornish peninsula, Wales, Northwest England and Scotland to the Pictish line and, of course, their stronghold, the Isle of Man.

The old Welsh chroniclers claim that of Britain 'the first of the three chieftains who established the colony was Hu, the Mighty, who came over with the original settlers. They crossed the hazy seas from the summer country which is called Deffrobani – that is where Constanoblys now stands'. Deffrobani is said to have been the name given to the glens of Albania between the Euxine and the Caspian seas.

Hu the Mighty is said to be identifiable with Lugh of the Irish and Llew or Lleu of the Welsh; he is, as we already know, the essential sun god. He is said to have obtained domination in Britain not by war or bloodshed but by justice and peace. He is credited with all the feats of the hero god; he slew a dragon; he caused the cessation of devastating floods; he federated people into tribes and taught them the art of agriculture as opposed to their former nomadic wanderings with cattle on the hoof as their wealth, and he was the first to draw a furrow with a plough on the soil of Britain. He is credited with having laid the foundations of literature and history by instituting Bardism and he is therefore called 'The First of the Three Pillars of the Isle of Britain'. He is indeed Arthur the Workman and Arthur the King returned in a new guise.

His labours approach those of Hercules in the Greek mysteries and his great feat was the drawing of the Avanc, a kind of giant Beaver, from the Lake and so delivering the country from its depredations – a feat which when taken symbolically is equivalent to releasing the land from the thrall of matter. There was a lifting up to the light above during the period of his sun sovereignty.

Unfortunately the exploits of Hu have not been written up and romanticized like that of Arthur and his Knights so that to the ordinary reader he is only a name – even if that; yet to anyone born in the West and inheriting the Western Tradition he should be a dear and familiar figure. He was the presiding god of the Mysteries for a long time and he developed the country on lines of peace and quiet settlement. He is the god of peace as well as of light.

The etymology of words is interesting. The Welsh word meaning Light or Lion is Llew. This is believed to be a corruption of El Hu, the Lord Hu or God Hu, Lord of Light – Light not only of the Sun, the benefactor of earth, but also of reason or mind, the light of the intelligence – the lord of the new period of evolution which was succeeding that of the intuition.

About 2000 BC the Assyrian word Ilu was the name for the Great God. The Keltic version is not very different when the march of centuries through Eastern Europe is considered. The Keltic word for Mind was Hew; in Chinese Hu stands for Sir or Lord, while the Christian name Hugh means mind or soul or spirit. There can be seen no real difference between Hugh and Llugh except a slight modification of the initial letter and a consequent simplification of pronunciation. In ancient Egyptian the word Knu may be broken down to Ek-Hu or Great Hu for, according to the British Museum Guide to the Egyptian Collection, this word 'Knu' means 'the shining translucent, transparent intangible essence of a man, and the word is on the whole best rendered by spirit'.

This same basic word can also be found in Mexico in the intricate god names of Juitzon and Huitsilopochtle. The ancient name of Mexico itself was Anahuec – which can quickly be seen to be an unusual combination of the Great Mother Ana and the Son Hu – and the word Huaca means either sacred or hill, showing the common belief that the gods dwelt usually in the high places. In this country Gloucester, Worcester and part of Warwickshire were once called Huiccas and were the territory of the Huicci.

Hu the Mighty Warrior was also the Keltic God of gentleness and he is still invoked to-day by mothers when they teach their children to say 'Gentle Iesu meek and mild', for it must be continually remembered that Jesus is a Keltic Western name and that the Hebrew form of it is Joshua. When they rock their babies to sleep and whisper 'Hushabye' the mothers are using a contraction for the old blessing 'May the light of Hu be with you'. The Bible translation of this universal wish for well being is to be found in the blessing 'The Lord make his face to shine upon thee'.

Jesus is a Keltic name and the God of the Gauls or Gaels was the counterpart Hesus. The Scandinavian version of the name is Aesir, and Aesar in Scandinavian mythology stands for the First Kindler or Creator; the Aesir Gods are the old gods, the forerunners and light bringers. All through the traditions therefore one comes to the first creating God who gives light and warmth, illumines the dark earth and causes the seed to fertilize and grow for the benefit of mankind. Aes, believed to be the very oldest form of the name and found in Gaul, is also to be found in the Persian Aser, the Hindu Aeswar, the Egyptian Asi (the Sun Bull) and in the Etruscan Asser. The Bhagavat Gita says of Aesar that 'he resides in every mortal'; he is indeed that indwelling Light of the World.

Light of the Mind is Wisdom and Understanding, and Hu is also therefore the Keltic God of Wisdom as well as the all pervading Sun. He and his worship have been perpetuated in strange ways – ways that come as a surprise to those who have not realized them. As was written in the chapter on the Horse and the Dragon, the Horse has been accepted throughout the ages in the West as the symbol of wisdom of the mind. Even at this time our judges' wigs are made of horsehair to symbolize the wisdom with which they have been endowed and are shaped in the form of the headdress of Mother Isis to show discernment. But they are called wigs, which is but a derivation from our own god Hu, who is the root of both wig and wise. Even to-day we can trace two great seats of his worship when we write to Wigtown and Wigan.

For the settlements of the Cymry stretched far beyond what is Wales to-day, though that became the last great centre of the Keltic worship. When the newer forms dominated the land, the old gods were driven up into the hills of Wales. That has been the last standing point of the desperate keepers of the past and it is significant that without perhaps knowing just why he used that allusion, Mr Churchill (as he then was) in his great speech of defiance in the war announced that if necessary the British would retreat to the hills of Wales before they would yield to the Nazis. Not, as might have been expected, to the Highlands of Scotland, but to the home of the great Keltic traditions, the holy places of the bygone centuries.

The lands of the Cymry stretched far beyond what is the principality of Wales today – up as far as Stirling in the Lowlands and across eastwards to Edinburgh, one of their strong places. The Scots came originally, it is believed, from Ireland, the descendants of Scota, wife of the Milesian king, and they settled in the West of Scotland and in South Wales, in the country round Pembroke, and it was here that the Hibernian and the Keltic mysteries intermingled and became that great mystery religion of Druidism.

Hu the Mighty was the lineal descendant of Arthur, whose mantle descended upon him, but behind him, great god as he was, was always the shadowy form of the old eternal Mother Goddess who gave birth to the world. The mother of the Gaelic Gods was known as the Mor-Rigan or the Great Mother – Her name is Anu – and the Morrigan as it is often spelt, can be easily broken up into the Gaelic Mohr, or Great, Rig or Righ the Leader or Queen – An – Anu.

Side by side with the worship of the Old Gods came the little known sect of the Culdees. They are believed to have been the direct descendants of the old Druids and to have been the bridge by which the gap between the old dispensation and the new was finally crossed. It is thought that they may have been a sort of sect of British monks or priests, unfriendly to the authority of Christian Rome and its discipline and retaining much of the Druid teaching. It has already been shown in the chapters on the Druids how easy was the transition between Druidism and Christianity. It has been suggested that their name was originally Cille De or Man of the Cell of God – i.e. monk or priest. In 1870 Dr John Jamieson published a work called *Historical Account of the Ancient Culdees of Iona* and says in the course of it that as late as 1850 there was a man in the parish of Moulin who never addressed the Supreme Being except as 'Arch-Druid', showing that the Druid priesthood was even a hundred years ago a living thing to the descendants of its tradition.

It has been said, also, though there can be no proof, that when Columba and his monks landed on Iona they were met by devils who tried to keep them from landing, and that these devils may well have been the members of an establishment of Culdees who quite understandably resented their presence.

Before St Augustine arrived in 597 there were Culdee settlements established in various parts of Britain. They were highly organized and disciplined, the monks labouring together in colleges, where they practised not only religion but music and the mechanical arts of the day. They did not observe canonical law except in so far as it fitted in with their conception of life, for they were permitted to marry. They had a hierarchy and the abbots of their colleges held office by hereditary right, so that we are able to trace that the Bishopric of Armagh was held by one family for fifteen generations.

Not unnaturally, the unorthodox practices caused the Church to take action against the Culdees, and in 813 they were denounced as heretics at the Second Council of Chalons, and three years later the Fifth Canon of the Council of Ceal Hythe forbade them to officiate as priests. But at the great church of St Andrew, in Fife, the Culdees, according to the Registry of the Priory of St Andrew 'continued to worship in a certain corner of the Church after their own manner, nor could this evil be removed till the time of Alexander of Blessed Memory'. Alexander of Blessed Memory did not reign in Scotland till 1124, so that for three hundred years the Culdees and the followers of the orthodox Roman Rite worshipped side by side in the same church, each priest conducting the mass according to his own ritual in a different part of the building.

In fairness to the Culdees, it should be noted that hereditary priesthood was not confined to their sect, but continued in Brittany in the regular Roman rite till 1127, and as late as 1200 Giraldus Cambrensis complains of it as a disgrace to Wales. Gradually it died out as the old conception of the priest-king was split into the two persons of the priest and the king, each functioning equally but separately, until they developed into the two great powers of Church and State.

That the Culdees were to some extent the successors of the Druids is a reasonable theory in view of the fact that the largest

Culdee settlements were found where the Druids are known to have been most strongly entrenched. There were Culdee monasteries at Ripon and at York until the days of Bede, and as late as 936 there was a Culdee colony attached to St Peter's, York. But their stronghold in Scotland was Iona until they were ousted by Columba.

In the course of years the western Mystery Schools of the early ages were absorbed into the Christian rite, but equally naturally some of their own teaching remained. The truism that 'plus ça change, plus c'est la même chose' is perhaps never more exemplified to the discerning than when it is connected with a change of religious faith. The Christian Church in the West, built, as we have seen, largely on what it found there; it transmuted the chief festivals into Church festivals; it did not try to destroy but to assimilate and to transform; it secured its results in fact on a basis of peaceful penetration; it turned Kings and Warriors into Saints and Holy Heroes; it threw out some of the more crude discrepancies but, generally speaking, where it could it redressed. In those early years it had already realized that you cannot utterly destroy and then rebuild; there you have the parable of the casting out of the devil and the re-entry of seven greater devils; a simple people will not endure the destruction of all that they have been taught to believe, neither will they believe that all that they have been taught is wrong and blasphemous; but they can be led gently but firmly to a new aspect of their old beliefs, which, founded on cosmic truths as all worth while religions must be, gradually take on the form of the new era and present a new façade to the rising generations. Even in this century regrets are often heard for the passing of 'old customs' such as 'wassail' and the 'Yule log' or the 'Mummers', kept up as curiosities in some parts of the country, but few customs could be more pagan and less Christian in their conception; with every regret at their passing we express our belief in the heritage which we have received from our Keltic forefathers and their expression of faith in the formulae of the Western Mysteries.

Certainly the Church attempted to suppress Druidism either by adjusting its salient features to a Christianity that could accept them without difficulty or, later on, by edict and command; to all outward form she succeeded. The Church has never taken kindly if at all to a divided authority, and by the time its teachings had taken a real hold of the people, the time had come for a change of mode and expression of faith; the age of Jesus the Christ had been fully inaugurated and it was right that at least as far as their outward observance was concerned the former things should pass away. Another step forward had to be taken in the evolution of the soul of man, but because a man takes another step forward he does not, if he is wise, discard that which has heretofore given him support; he leaves it behind him eventually, but with gratitude, seeing how far it has brought him and how its essence is still mingled with the new stand which he has naturally achieved. The wise man recognizes the ladder which has helped him to climb and is careful to retain its integral support lest his last stage be worse than his first.

How long did the mystery teaching continue under the old name of Druidism? In the more remote parts of the countries no doubt for many centuries. Progress comes slowly to isolated places and to islands cut off from the mainland for many months of the year. News of the newer rites would not only penetrate slowly but would be slowly received by those who had already proved the efficacy of their older beliefs. In Ireland, the earliest known writings refer to the Science of Goibmui, a master of Druidic magic, and to the 'healing of Dianecht', the god of Medicine, and these references can be found in MSS of the eighth and ninth centuries AD and in use for magical purposes in Christian times. In Ireland the magicians' wands are known as the Rods of Druidism'. Among the Kelts, the word Druid signifies Wizard as well as Holy or Blessed Man, and in the Welsh Bible, Simon Magus is translated as Simon the Druid. Rhys says that Simon became known to the Church as a bitter opponent of the Apostles and his name was therefore associated with everything that was considered pagan. Magus and Druid may be taken as synonymous terms in the minds of those who were at that period trying to separate the sheep from the goats.

Gwalchmai the Bard between 1150 and 1290, wrote an elegy on Madoc Prince of Powys which cried 'Would to God the day of doom were arrived since Druids are come bearing the news of woe.' And his contemporary, Cynddlew, in his panegyric on Owen

Gwynedd says 'Bards are constituted the judges of excellence, and bards will praise thee, even Druids of the circle, of four dialects, coming from the four regions.' Elsewhere he speaks also of 'Druids of the splendid race, wearers of the God chains', and in another poem he says 'It is commanded by the Druids of the land that songs be prepared', and later refers to himself as 'A bard of Keridwen, the mystic goddess.'

The acceptance of Christianity did not mean the abandonment of the Druid philosophy. One triad says 'There are three special doctrines that have been obtained by the nation of the Cymry; the first from the age of ages was that of the Gwynddoniad, prior to the time of Prydain, the son of Aedd the great; the second was Bardism, as taught by the Bards after they had been instituted; and the third was the Faith in Christ, being THE BEST OF THE THREE.'

Many Druids became Christian priests, finding it easy to assimilate the rites and beliefs of the early Church since of their own wisdom they could perceive that the foundations of all forms of religion are basically the same. So anxious was the Church that the 'conversion' should be carried through and so aware was it of the fundamental similarity that a Bull of Pope Gregory I (540-604) permitted the fusion of the Druid and Christian beliefs.

The first Christian school founded in these islands was that of St Illtyd or Llan-Illtyd-Fawr, which was begun in 508. It was a famous school and among its pupils it numbered such outstanding persons as St David Gildas, Bishop Paulinus and Archbishop Sampson.

The glory of the Druids decayed, as all glories must, and the remnants of their faith went underground until the next revival of religion should call for its release and it should be needed for the forthcoming age.

But as late as 1538 the rites of Hu Gadarn were being celebrated, which means that a priest was working the esoteric mysteries of the old Western traditions up to four hundred years ago, for the power and the knowledge must have been handed on through the centuries or there would have been no succession to make the ritual potent. In a letter from one Ellis Price to Thomas Cromwell, dated 6 April 1538 it is stated that an image of Hu

Gadarn was being held up as a goal of pilgrimage and offerings. To kill this dangerous revival of the cult, the Church acted swiftly; the image was taken to Smithfield in that same year and publicly burnt. That was an understandable action but there is more to it than that. According to the record with the image was burned *a friar of the same name.* Now no monk of any of the orthodox Roman orders would have been so treated, even if he had so forgotten himself as to set up as an idol worshipper, so that the word 'friar' must connote something different. Who would bear the same name as the god save the priest working the rite of the god on whom through the ages the power of the god had descended that he might become the interpreter of the wisdom to the worshippers?

Professor Sir John Rhys was convinced that the hereditary priesthood in Wales survived at least to the beginning of the twentieth century, and in proof of this he cites the case of the Well of the Oxen at St Teilo. Here there is a well in the churchyard, the water of which is considered remedial for whooping-cough but it must be drawn from the well in a skull – now said to be that of St Teilo himself – and given to the patient by some member of the family born in the adjoining house, preferably by the eldest son and heir. Oxen have, of course, been the sacred beasts of Hu Gadarn throughout the centuries; the corruption of St Teilo is open to speculation, but one may suppose that he was not always a Christian saint, and when it transpires that the family have occupied the same house for hundreds of years and that their name is Melchior, it is not very difficult to see that the hereditary rights over the well and the hereditary priesthood are not far separated.

As late as the seventeenth century the Cauldron of Keridwen was associated with a revival of the Druid faith in Scotland. In 1871, well into the reign of Queen Victoria and the prominence of Balmoral and the tartan and the cairns, the Revd James Rust, minister of Slains, published a work called *Druidism Exhumed;* in this he pointed out that only a hundred years before then the General Assembly of the Church of Scotland was persuaded that Druidism was being practised all over the country and took drastic steps to put an end to it.

Mr Rust also mentioned that on Bennachie in Aberdeenshire there is a slope called the Great Cauldron Ascent, and a stone called the Very Great Cauldron Stone, from which the Cauldron itself has been removed. The Cauldron, one might surmise, was the upper stone of a rocking stone, which has been either actually removed or has fallen from its base during the passing of time.

The Cauldron is missing but on the stone itself is cut a figure which Mr Rust considered to be a representation of it and says 'It is the holy Caldron, the Caldron of Knowledge and Initiation, for it has the Z figure running through it.' This Z figure is sometimes called the Broken Spear or the Broken Sceptre. Lewis Spence considers it to represent the zigzag lightning from Heaven, the Flaming Sword, which the Qabalists call the Lightning Flash.

These are small illustrations of practising Druidism through the centuries but sufficiently documented to show how the work of the Mysteries has never died. In the hearts of the faithful they have been deeply engraved and those who have served them in the past are returning to take up their old work and serve them again in their newer form. It needs but the touch of the right spring from them to leap out again into the open as did the contents of Pandora's Box.

Chapter 12

And now...

An outline, brief indeed, but yet perhaps more connected than others which may have gone before it, now lies behind you. This is the story of your inheritance as a member of the Western world. Far be it from me to ask or to suggest that any one should discard the teaching in which he has found contentment and realization of his higher self. But for those who are still seeking, who are not yet at one with their inner lives, let them consider whether this is not the way that they have not known, the path on which they should tread. For it is their heritage.

Fiona Macleod wrote: 'There is no law set upon beauty; it has no geography. It is the domain of the spirit. And if, of those who enter there, peradventure any comes again, he is welcome for what he brings; nor do we demand if he be dark or fair, Latin or Teuton or Kelt, or say of him that his tidings are lovelier or less lovely because he was born in the shadow of Gaelic hills or nurtured by Keltic shores. It is well that each should learn the mother song of his land at the cradle place of his birth ... But it is not well that because of the whistling of the wind in the heather one should imagine that nowhere else does the wind suddenly stir the reeds and the grasses in its incalculable hour.'

This is your inheritance, you who are born of the West, whether you like to admit it or not. And it is only right that having been told something about it, you should consider how it is applicable to you – what do you propose to do to further its work in the world?

There are the Mystery Schools of the West as well as of the East; they are alive and working to-day in circumstances which permit a student to work and yet carry on in his profession or trade, for the West is ever practical and knows that the purely mystic type of life is suitable and possibly only for the few. No good ever came of neglecting the responsibilities already undertaken for the sake of advancement in the Mysteries. The responsibilities may have been assumed lightly, may be regretted, but they must be considered and grappled with as a part of the discipline that goes with every step towards the higher way of living. There is no blessing for the man who neglects his work in this incarnation for what he thinks is the better and the quicker way forward.

If you are in need of a Mystery School and of a teacher to show you the way, one will be sent when you are ready to receive him. That when a man is ready the teacher will come is true; I have proved it for myself; if the teacher does not come, the answer is that, whatever he may think, the pupil is not yet ready for the next step. It may be that he has even to learn a lesson of elementary patience and faith; it may be that he has not yet done for himself all that he can in the way of preparation. It is the duty of the pupil to be prepared; it is not the duty of the teacher to waste valuable time on preliminary instruction; when the teacher comes, the lessons should begin at once; the schoolroom must be swept and garnished and the previous lessons and examinations faithfully learnt and honestly experienced.

Here again we are so likely to be faced with the difficulties of our modern Western civilization; of the age of speed in which we are of necessity living; we are so eager to make progress and we so often reckon that progress by what we see with the outward eye, forgetting that, like icebergs, nine-tenths of it should be within the heart and unseen by mortal men. It is the ultimate results that count, the cleansing of the heart and mind of pride and desire, not the ability to recite formulae and work rituals.

In no case perhaps is it more necessary to make haste slowly than in the choice of a Mystery School. Before presenting oneself at its doors for enrolment, so much has to be considered and weighed; a wrong step at this first stage can have far-reaching consequences and may throw one back for at least the balance of this incarnation. In making this important decision, various factors ought to be considered. In almost all – if not all – of the mystery schools an obligation is required of secrecy to the outer world of that which may be communicated within it. It is therefore necessary to be quite sure of the integrity of those with whom one will be working, for occult vows have powerful and far-reaching consequences when they are broken and it is a terrible thing to have to choose between being forsworn and conniving at malpractices. Schools of sound repute are to be found; their pupils speak well of them when asked in confidence; and while no initiate will betray a secret yet the genuine seeker for knowledge will find a ready response to fair and reasonable inquiries. Again, when the soul is ready, the teacher or the friend will appear.

There is no secret about the fact that I was trained for many years by the late Dion Fortune, Warden of the Society (then the Fraternity) of the Inner Light. I had known her long before over a matter of business and had lost touch with her for perhaps ten years. I was looking for the guide whom I knew would be sent when I was ready; I had been waiting for some months, still trying to prepare myself, having faith that when the time came the word would be sent. Without any warning at all, Dion Fortune came into my office one day and remarked after our discussion that she was now Warden of the Fraternity (of which I had not even heard) and that she was giving three public lectures on Ceremonial Magic, beginning that evening, and would I care to come and hear her. My teacher had been sent and I knew then that all my months of faith and work were to be rewarded.

There is a fundamental rule among occultists of standing that the occult arts must never be used for gain, and this again is a criterion which may be applied when choosing a school. A fair fee to cover overhead expenses is and should be asked; there is no reason why the mystery schools should be charitable organizations dependent on the whims and generosity of a few; they are entitled to be supported in their outward and visible form, as indeed they must be if they are to flourish, since in this country neither the temperature nor the climate permit of free instruction under a palm tree and rent and rates and taxes for accommodation have to be found. But the school which persists in asking directly or indirectly for lavish gifts for the benefit of the leaders is not likely to offer very much in the way of worth while occult knowledge and may lead the neophyte into very deep waters.

Taking it as a general rule, it is wisest to keep to the foundations which belong to the traditions in which one was born at the particular time. It might surely be taken for granted that the Lords of Karma know what is best for each of us and a man born into the West has probably need of the mystery teaching of this hemisphere – if only for one incarnation – in order that he may learn something which would otherwise be outside his experience.

But whatever may be the outcome, into whatever form of the Mysteries you decide to apply to become a worker, you must take your initiation into a system and become *conditioned* to its symbols before you can use it and work with its exponents.

This is an axiom which is not always remembered by the younger brethren who become deeply interested in the Eastern teaching. They are not by virtue of birth and upbringing naturally conditioned to it already, and much time and energy has to be expended in getting this state of affairs into a proper perspective. This not unnaturally is liable to lead to disappointment and dissatisfaction; it is as though one were attempting to become a citizen of an alien country without first experiencing the conditions of living, the legislation, even the language. Unless there is any sound reason to the contrary, surely it is better to stand by one's own? The country which was responsible for the infant nurture is probably the one in which one is intended to work.

Each nation has not only its own group soul but its own group mind – something which is not always remembered or recognized; and this group mind is the gateway to the group soul. If you will think carefully on this statement, it will be clear how important it is for the group mind to be understood before the attempt is made to contact the group soul. You must learn a language before you can begin to communicate in the idiom of a country.

You may say – and with truth – that there is a common group soul; a group soul which is shared by all human beings since all are part of the same type of evolution, but this participation in that which is common to all does not give you the right of entry into the private lands of a certain section, any more than, one might say, being an Old Boy of a school gives you the right of entry into a

Club which is restricted by certain conditions of membership to certain grades of qualified Old Boys. If you wish to adopt a system which is not your own by right of birth and circumstances, then you have to be tested and conditioned by a member of the group practising that system, and after a considerable period of preliminary training be directly initiated into that national system.

And let me remind you again that it is indeed a *national* system and that, although in the higher regions of all occult work there are no nations and no creeds in the mystery schools, yet basically their presentation of the universal teaching and their ritual and outlook are formed by the circumstances in which they have been founded.

That is pure common-sense. 'God fulfils Himself in many ways'; we are not all alike; we are not meant to be all alike; only when we have reached that rare stage of super-personality can we stand outside all our human ties and relationships and dispositions and be completely above and beyond such contacts. And those who are called upon and are capable of reaching such heights might, one would suggest, be numbered upon the fingers of one hand during each series of incarnations. For the general run of us it is better to accept the conditions which the Lords of Karma have seen fit to impose on us for this incarnation at any rate, remembering that if we have even so slightly turned our faces steadfastly towards Jerusalem, we have been allowed to cooperate with the Ministers of God to the extent of asking permission to be sent back towards the fulfilment of our destiny – that One-ness with the Divine to which in our secret hearts we all aspire, knowing that one day all of us will reach his Feet.

One more word on this point. When an initiate of the mystery schools comes back here again to work, he hears the call of his former school and his immediate instinct is to return to the group of which he had once been a part and to which he is bound by the inner ties. Life after life the initiates of the Ancient Mysteries hear the call and find their way back to the Temple in which their co-initiates are working on this plane of matter. This is the secret of the genuine mystery schools working successfully to-day: the greater number of their members are their own old initiates who have come back prepared in the inner planes to take up the work as soon as the leader gives the call; as soon as the teacher has begun the work of rebuilding the outer manifestations of the Inner Temple. When that is in hand the clarion call goes out on the inner planes and the subconscious and superconscious minds are stirred and gradually the co-workers come together again – strangely dissimilar perhaps in their material forms and their material outlook, but nevertheless, as Kipling has it, 'Fellow craftsmen, no more and no less.'

Temples pass away; the form of the work has to be changed to suit the conditions of evolution; but the teachers come back to hand down the knowledge of the inner courts and to lead into them those members of the outer rooms who have now gained the right of entry into the middle chambers.

It is noticeable that during the twentieth century the uprush of mystery teaching has been enormously greater than in the previous years – new schools of Higher Thought, new suggestions for becoming something a little out of the ordinary in the matter of spiritual development; teaching for the release of the Super-Consciousness – all these and parallel offers may be found over the Western world, and perhaps more especially in the United States. Why is this? If the Mystery Schools are all that we have claimed that they are, why were they driven underground for so long? Why has our Western teaching, which we have shown to be of immemorial age been neglected for hundreds of years except by a few of the faithful? Why has it been so necessary to resurrect and reconstruct the Mystery Schools in order that the hungry sheep may look up and be fed – and, as an original question, why are they hungry?

It is one of these developments which has to be taken in the light of whole periods of evolution; our tendency is to consider a few hundred years a long time instead of acquiring the viewpoint that it is indeed a minute period in the Day of Creation.

As has been said before in this book, it is essential that the old order should change; refusal to change has been the ruin of more than one religion and will probably be the ruin of many more. More than one aspect of the Mystery Teachings has been faded out from above because the exponents of it here did not 'move with the times', modify their teaching and generally progress in the outer while keeping the inner mysteries inviolate. Fifty years ago in some of the Mystery Schools vows of deepest secrecy were taken concerning things which are now the commonplace of science; radio, the discovery of atomic energy, the countless mechanical and scientific developments of the last half century have rendered futile and rather ridiculous the taboos of many older forms of obligation as well as embarrassing the neophyte who finds that he is pledged to solemn secrecy on something which he has known about for a long time in the outer world. A true Mystery School must concern itself with the hidden mysteries in their essentials and appreciate that as the period of evolution grows; so the mysteries of the past which were marvels of hidden magic become the commonplaces of the present and may be rejected as out-of-date in the light of greater discoveries as science develops.

But the fundamental truths do not change. It is that which lies behind these tremendous manifestations which is the concern of the Mystery Teaching.

The central home of learning was at one time the Euphrates Valley. Here the great Mystery Colleges were broken up and dispersed by Alexander the Great, when he descended upon them with his armies. No doubt at the time, this seemed to those concerned to be the end of all Light, but viewed in the dispassionate microscope of a more distant time it was by no means the tragedy it appeared. Numbers of priests were driven out into the world and they took with them an esoteric knowledge which had up till that moment been denied to those outside the orbit. As the course of evolution was planned, this great exodus took place just at the time when the move towards individualism was beginning; when men were taking hold of their own characters and developing them from the herd in which they had been nourished; they were beginning to think each man for himself and not necessarily bound to work in highly ordered and specialized groups. The day of the individual man in his glory is the day when each man is the controller of his own destiny in accordance with the Divine Will. That was the beginning of that future dream.

Naturally the work of the groups was not entirely dispersed among single priests, travelling and teaching independently, but it was changed in character; the knowledge was spread over a much greater portion of the globe and more and more men became initiates. In spite of the break up of the great Colleges the desire for union was still strong; the group habit was a development of the herd instinct and a fundamental characteristic then as now. Temples were formed and Schools were inaugurated because there was this great need among men for the strong to protect the less strong; a collegia or sodality was formed to give all men in the group the protection of its unity; these sodalities usually met and performed certain rites devised by their leaders in order to give them individuality and a password and ritual that would enable them to detect the outsider; frequently they were linked to temples which honoured certain deities and then the rites became connected with the deities.

As time went by, some of these groups became more strongly religious in their outlook and became the nuclei of brotherhoods or mystery schools; others laid more stress on the well being of their members in the material world and developed into guilds and unions. Many of the mystery schools in the old days may be traced to such sources. The essence of a Mystery School is that it should be founded with the intent to practise the Mysteries, with a leader at the head of it who has taken the necessary initiations and can then confer the required degrees upon others – and so the wisdom of the ages is handed down.

Gradually the State religions failed to hold the more educated members of the populace. As the Greek and then the Roman Empires became more and more formalized and stylized so the 'outward and visible' signs took a more prominent part in the rituals until the inner meanings were almost forgotten and certainly their significance unappreciated by a very large number of the participants. Not unnaturally the Deification of an Emperor did not secretly impress his former boon companions, though it was not advisable for them to admit it even in secret. Inevitably the more intelligent members of a State drew away; the growth of individualization could not stomach the unmeaning formality from which the spirit had departed; there was either atheism, disbelief, or however it might be defined, of which perhaps the most elevated school was that of the Stoics, or there was a seeking for the Mysteries, the unappeasable hunger which asserts itself when the fleshpots have failed to sustain life.

With the coming of individualization came the Stoic term 'conscience', the inward knowledge of a man of himself. Seneca has written: 'Every day I plead my case before myself. When the light is extinguished and my wife, who knows my habit, keeps silent, I examine the past day, do over and weigh all my deeds and words. I hide nothing; I omit nothing. Why should I hesitate to face my short-comings when I can say "Take care not to repeat them and so I forgive you today"?'

What is this but the earliest form of the training in self-examination of a modern Mystery School? 'Know Thyself' is the first commandment in the teaching of the initiate. Only by knowing oneself can one command the essential humility and courage of straightforward thought which alone can take the veils from our eyes and expose the bright shining Truth.

It is interesting and instructive to note how when the work of an era has been completed the mysteries are driven underground until the next cycle is started. Here as everywhere else, there must it seems be the period of germination, while the world is required to assimilate and make use of that which it has already been given; to progress to a point at which it is possible it might be able to appreciate a new truth, a new aspect of the essential story. Alexander broke up the Colleges in the Euphrates Valley; the great Western Mystery Schools were broken up again and again, usually by the Church of Rome – as at the time of that great massacre of the Templars about 1306. After that a long period of silence – long that is from the view of the men of this world but infinitesimally short when compared with the evolution of the whole – and then the last recrudescence in the middle of the nineteenth century.

About a hundred years ago the first stirrings of the New Age were heard, an Age which came to blossom then and is opening now, one believes, into full flower. How long this period may continue we do not know, and it is not for us to speculate. But it is for us so to conduct ourselves that when we shall have passed out of this mortal dream into the real life beyond, we shall be ready to return to the duty of perfecting our own evolution and bringing it nearer to that ultimate return to God which is essential before the realization of God Himself can be completed; when next we are faced with the onus and burden of incarnation, let us at least be able to come back with the awareness that we shall be meeting once more those with whom we have worked countless times in the past and shall meet countless times in the future and be prepared to take our places in the classrooms of our own Mystery Schools there to learn the lessons we omitted to prepare before, and, if we be called upon to do so, to fit ourselves to pass on the teaching to the younger souls who have not yet taken their initiation.

Let us always remember that the power behind the Mystery Schools is the power of the Divine passing into manifestation. The Mystery Schools throughout the ages have known how to build and prepare the channels through which the Divine Power is manifested; the Power itself does the rest; it is the duty of the workers in the Schools to prepare the ground. 'I planted; Apollos watered; but God gave the increase.' So spoke a great Teacher who knew that man is but the instrument; the Divine Power is the Force; but there must be an instrument for manifestation. The Mystery Schools and their initiates are but the instruments of a mighty and conscious and intelligent Will, which is ultra human, as we understand the word – transcending superhuman consciousness.

The Mystery Gods were never immaterial ghosts or spiritual essences in human form, nor were they material idols, as the Church has tried to make them out to be in the teachings of its Darker Ages. They were as much a part of the One God as the wave is part of the sea; each named God is but a named wave, an aspect of the Divine and unbreakable whole. But since the gods, like the waves, are formless energies, it was necessary for man to personalize them in the shape of images that he might have the necessary form into which to pour the engendered force, since uncontrolled force is useless. And when man is bringing the force of the Divine Energy into play upon this world, then it is obvious that he must be able to direct and control it in a form comprehensible to himself and to his co-worshippers. This is the reason for the tremendous force of the godlike images, built to pattern throughout the ages by the initiated priests. This is why it is so important that when making a god-image for the purpose of using it as a channel for power you should know the details of the portrait; the attributes; the colours and the shapes; else if you get a distorted picture the power cannot flow freely through it; the picture that you are striving to make is one that has been made in the same form throughout the ages and it is not for you to tamper with the agreed design; if you do the failure of your practical work will be attributable only to you.

That is again another reason why the would-be initiate should remain in so far as possible with his own group and his own way of living. If he attempts to participate in a group mind that is alien to him, he will find that although he may understand it, he can neither practise it nor use the technique to any good effect. He is not, strictly speaking, a member; the group mind of the school is a sealed book. He must take his initiation in what is to him a new tradition and this is one reason – and the chief one – why, ordinarily speaking, so few Europeans are able to use the great Oriental traditions of China, India and Thibet. These do not come naturally to them and a fresh start has to be made, whereas they may be as giants in their own land. It is also interesting to see that, again speaking generally, foreigners can seldom take their full training in a school working with the English group soul. They can be trained to a certain point in meditation and in psychology and also in the philosophy and comparative methods of the Mysteries. But when it comes to the practical work with a team using the rituals it will be discovered that, as a rule, their work is weak; there is a link which is not formed, illusory, and which cannot be forged.

The Temples of the Order in the physical world may be broken down; the churches of this dispensation of the Christ of Love may kill or suppress every initiate belonging to the Temples; but the Mystery Temple on the inner planes cannot be destroyed and no power on earth or in so-called Heaven can prevent the reincarnation of the initiates and their intuitive recovery of the knowledge of the mysteries which they have gleaned in past incarnations.

All mystery systems, all metaphysical philosophy, all religion that is more than a formal expression of a series of dogmas or an ethical expression of herd law, are nothing more or less than systems of props whose sole object is to support and to steady the human mind while it slowly prepares itself for the final plunge into Thrice Greatest Darkness, which is the Ineffable Light, which is in very truth, Nirvana – At-one-ness with the Supreme Life.

Chapter 13

how to Enjoy your heritage

It is obvious that where the teaching of the Mysteries is concerned there must be above all things a firm and practical basis on which to build, or the whole of the system will fall down and be confused in what has been so aptly described as 'muzzy mysticism', a state of mind which is good for neither man nor woman, which leads to confusion of the planes, to a misinterpretation of symbols and to a general dissatisfaction and occasional actual harm to the student worker. The word occasional is used here advisedly because the practice of the mysteries is so exact a science that if indifferently or carelessly performed the results are not usually sufficiently positive to do real damage but merely result in a feeling of malaise and a dismayed conviction that it is all rather silly and futile and that there is 'nothing to it'.

Nothing could in truth be further from the actual facts. Properly studied and with the practical work carefully supervised and handled, the Mysteries are as satisfying and fruitful as any other science can be to the worker. But they are no more suitable for the practice of every one than are astronomy or engineering or poetry for those who have no aptitude; no harm comes of the labour but it is unrewarding. Owing to the amount of rather inexpert fanciful literature on the subject, there is a tendency to believe that 'magic' can be worked by any one from an amateur fortune teller to a 'black magician'; in theory of course this is true, but in practice it is certainly a misapprehension. It is as hard to produce practical results in magic if you are not trained for the work as it is to produce a satisfactory soufflé when your own culinary accomplishment stops short at boiling an egg.

The German philosopher, Gustav Fechner, has set out in the course of his theological speculations the basis on which the practical training of a mystery school has been set up. Unfortunately Fechner himself has not, so far as I know, been translated completely into English; on the other hand, as with many German writers of his type and period, he tends to overload his theme with material. In his work *A Pluralistic Universe* William James has given us the Fechner philosophy. Even this book however, is stiffer reading than many a beginner will wish to tackle, though it does eventually repay the labour involved.

The first requisite in the first stage of the training of an initiate is KNOW THYSELF. This is something which presents great difficulty to many people, for it involves the complete impersonal approach and unemotional view of their own standing, beliefs and desires which a number of would-be students cannot bring themselves to face. No one would suggest it is a pleasant experience but it is essential to start the work on a perfectly honest foundation. To know oneself in the eyes of God is never an easy thing to do. It requires a complete purgation, a catharsis, a breaking down of the barriers between the personality and the individuality so that the veils of pretence are stripped from the real motives they conceal. It is moreover a treatment which may have to be repeated many times; even with the best will in the world it is not always possible to tear away the trappings on a first occasion and there is a point where it may be wiser to retreat in order to return when the first shock is over and the will to proceed is renewed. The point at which the ordinary man cannot stand self-exposure but turns away in dismay or even horror at the sight of his real self is one that is reached at different stages by different people, but there are few if any who do not have to beat a retreat the first time, at any rate, to preserve the remnants of pride and save the ultimate shame. But if a man is an earnest student and determined to gain the truth of the Mysteries and not merely to linger on the outer fringe, he will have the courage and the strength and endurance to complete this basic work, though it may take a long time; even, by our standards, days, months, and even years. But one thought may bring him a grain of comfort. This ultimate facing of what we really are, this putting of our real self and our self-believed self vis-a-vis is something which we shall have to confront without respite or relief when we find ourselves beyond the gate of death; if we have had the courage and the sense to cope with the situation in this life, there is one trial that will be either spared us or immensely lightened on the other side.

Having reached this goal and stripped ourselves of worldly desires and emotions and become the genuine individuals that lie behind the personalities, what comes next? A goal appears which is almost equally hard to face; the question which each student must then ask himself is WHAT DO I KNOW? Not what do I believe, nor what have I been taught – but what do I KNOW? It is a pre-requisite for the genuine seeker for the Mysteries that he shall be able to think for himself. That is why the rich young man came to Jesus and was allowed to go away sorrowful. He was not ready to leave the herd, to throw over his knowledge, much as it was, his beliefs and his tenets, and to stand on his own feet and find himself perhaps in opposition to those with whom he had worked and studied before. Know Thyself, combined with a decision as to what one does actually know, makes the first step on the path to true knowledge of the Mysteries.

And now comes the second stage; the completion of those two pointers of the way. KNOW THYSELF THROUGH THYSELF. This is a great Mystery and a hard saying and an even harder thing to put into practice. For this is that period of desolation when all else is stripped away and the initiate finds that he and he alone is God to himself.

This stage is known throughout the Mystery Schools of the world under various names; in the West it is usually referred to as the Mystery of the Empty Tomb or Pastos. It is hinted at in the Gospel story when on Easter morning they came to the Sepulchre and found it empty. In the ancient Egyptian ceremonies it was the culmination of a long period of study and training; the initiate was led from temple to temple, each one presided over by the power of a God more potent, more abstract than the one previously encountered; and then at last he was led in darkness to the Holy of Holies and when the bandage was taken from his eyes he found before him nothing but an empty chamber furnished with an empty sarcophagus. Here there was no presiding power; it was his own kingdom; here he had to learn that ultimately he must rely solely and utterly upon himself; not upon his personality or his individuality; not on the pitiful pride of his earthly competence, but upon his own higher self, his knowledge of his union with the Supreme Being, and his awareness that within his limited capacity he was indeed himself the Supreme Being. Here he discovered that he alone could illumine the Temple, light the lamp in the sanctuary that would bring brilliance out of the darkness, place himself in the empty sarcophagus and know himself to be indeed at one with God.

This was the tremendous lesson of the God Within. As it is written in the Gospel of St John: 'At that day ye shall know that I am in my Father, and ye in me, and I in you.'

Now you may perhaps understand why it is said that there is so much hard work involved in training for the Mysteries. But remember, however, that this is not a training which a man is expected to complete in one incarnation, nor two, nor even in a dozen. It is a stage or state of progression throughout the ages; to some it may come sooner than to others; to some it may seem permanently withheld, but it will eventually be reached by all those who set their faces steadfastly towards Jerusalem.

Do not overlook the importance of that word Steadfastly; it is the key to the life of the Mysteries which is the life with the Supreme Being, the life hidden in God. Delay and destruction and disappointment come to those who have set their hands to the plough and have turned back; no one urges you forward; no one asks you to increase the pace which you have set yourself; but if you have once elected to go to Jerusalem the failure to go forward, even at a snail's pace, is a failure to yourself, to your own higher being and ultimately a failure towards God.

How often do we hear kindly and charitable people say of some one that he is his own worst enemy – meaning that he cannot control himself or make the most of the opportunities given to him; never could this be more truly said than of those who desire to know of the Mysteries and halt by the wayside, desiring but not making the effort to obtain knowledge because the price is too great for them to pay. The work demands a tremendous effort at one point of the road or another, but once the decision to go forward has been taken and the first step covered in all humility and with the realization of what it may – indeed must – involve, then in all difficulties and trials and dangers there is a strong sweet voice coming from within, still pointing the way to the morning star and the city set on the hill, and reminding the aspirant that the reward is so much greater than the cost of gaining it.

Truth must be brought into use in every stage of the mystery teaching and the mystery working, for Truth is the great reward of the Mysteries; Truth who lives at the bottom of a well. And what is that well but the magic mirror, the reflection of that which is above? We have learnt already of the importance of the well, of still water, of the reflective possibilities of a smooth polished surface. But Truth at the bottom of the well is not always attractive to the eye of the man at the top; uncompromisingly she shows just what is there; each blemish, each scar, each wound is faithfully reflected. The man who can face Truth without flinching, and use what she tells him for the improvement of his work in life, has gone a good way upon the path that leads to the fulfilment of the promise of the Mysteries.

In his work *Pragmatism,* William James writes: 'Truth lives in fact for the most part on a credit system. Our thoughts and beliefs 'pass' so long as nothing challenges them, just as banknotes pass so long as nobody refuses them. But all this points to direct face to face verification somewhere without which the fabric of truth collapses like a financial system with no cash basis whatever. You accept my verification for one thing, I yours for another. We trade on each other's truth. But beliefs verified concretely by *somebody* are the posts of the whole super-structure.'

This principle is the foundation of all training; the posts must be verified by somebody, and it is important when taking up training to know by whom and from whom this verification comes. In every Mystery School it must and should be possible to verify the truth and accuracy of the system used. This can be done by proof on the inner planes; the outward and visible forms can be given and checked, but ultimately it comes back to the individual worker in the field. I KNOW THROUGH MYSELF because I have experienced and because I have so trained and developed my faculties that I can trust the inner knowledge given to me to be pure and undefiled and untainted by worldly desire, emotion or pride. That is the standard at which the student of the Mysteries must aim.

As soon as he is qualified in any Mystery School the initiate should proceed to verify the system by which he has been taught. Always in the end it comes to the same point; the requirement that the initiate must initiate himself. This is the crucial moment of his life in the Mysteries. The Gnosis or Knowingness of 'ten thousand times great Hermes', as Zosimus calls him, is the goal. The Hermetic Initiation is based on two principles, called in Greek, Theosophia or the Wisdom or Knowledge of God, and Theosabia, which may be translated as Worship of the Religion of the Mind, which the ancients called the Bread of Wisdom.

Knowledge is never gained except by sacrifice; there is a price to be paid for everything that is worth having. It is when he has got to this stage and has reached the point where he can truly say that he has begun to know, and has proved the path on which he proposes to walk, that the young initiate has to make up his mind as to his future course. Now there lies before him the prospect of work in so many directions; so much is open to his selection; all of it is thrilling, absorbing and greatly needed. But he cannot hope to touch all even in passing; there is but one lifetime before him in which to work in the world before he is called to assimilate that which he has learnt and to distil its essence while he is resting between his periods of incarnation.

It is at this stage that the decision must be taken as to which system is the one to which his mind should be given. He must now decide what he wants and what he is prepared to pay to get it. And as has been suggested all through this book, the most suitable system for the Westerner is the Western Tradition. But whichever is selected, it means throwing overboard the symbology and phraseology of the others; he must fill his mind with one set of images and one set of names and be prepared to test that system thoroughly. To confuse symbols and planes is to court disaster; to correlate them on the Tree of Life is good, for it enables him to assess them at their correct valuation and to see how all work together to the same end; but the actual practical work should be confined to the one set of symbols and all temptation to use the others must be set aside for a much later date in the journey of progress. As has been said earlier on, an initiate is conditioned into the requirements of a system and it is therefore manifestly clear that having got so far he should work on the lines of that system, once he has proved it to be satisfactory.

Having concentrated upon this stage, and having learned his lesson in one school, the student will later on be able, as says the Eastern Commentary on a sacred writing, 'to brush the star dust with his lips from the Lotus Feet of the great Mother of all'. And there is more in this phrase than a merely beautiful poetic expression, for the Symbol of the Two Feet is a symbol of possession or visitation. The Feet of Osiris formed one of the portions of his dismembered body and are always referred to in the plural. In the *Book of the Dead* it is said, 'I have come upon earth and with my two feet have taken possession. I am Tmu.' The symbol is universal. It is found in India, carved on rocks, on dolmens in Brittany and on rock carvings in Scandinavia, and everywhere the meaning is the same; the God has come and has been recognized by His own. In Ireland the reference has naturally been Christianized and is applied to St Patrick or to St Columba. Even in Mexico, that opposite number, so to speak, of the Egyptian culture, the symbolism is found. In *Primitive Culture* Tyler refers to 'the Aztec ceremony at the Second Festival of the Sun God, when they sprinkled maize flour before his sanctuary and his high priest watched till he beheld the divine footprints and then shouted to announce "Our Great God is Come".'

The Initiate is now standing on the threshold of the next and third stage – when he is actually preparing to work the Mysteries. This stage of consciousness carries with it its own difficulties and its own temptations. So many are apt to mistake conscious knowledge for consciousness of life. Conscious knowledge might be defined as the fruit of experience in this material world. To become conscious of Life and the Life Force you must be able to stand beneath the Tree of Life and pluck its Fruit for yourself.

In the older mystery teachings of all countries and systems and even in some of the exponents of today, it was considered essential that the initiate should construct his own magical weapons with his own hands and by the sweat of his brow. To-day it is not essential that an initiate should be able to carve, to work metal and to forge.

In the earlier and more primitive times this was the outward and visible sign of his zeal and his endurance and also emphasized the fact that in the work of the Mysteries there can be no mass production. A man must be himself and must make his own tools. But to-day the symbolism of the outward tools may be taken in its inner meaning of personal knowledge. The tools are the focusing points of the power which is used in the work; they are not the essentials. There is as much power in the pointed finger as in the dagger, providing the motivating force behind is working truly. The real meaning is that every initiate must fill his mind with the right magical images, correctly pictured; that he must know them intimately so that at any moment he can call up the correct form and colour and attributes; that is another reason why the Mysteries are for the few rather than for the many, since they demand creative artists upon the inner planes, prepared to combine and re-combine until the right answer is achieved.

Creative reading again is different from ordinary reading and should form part of the work of the student. In creative reading the student takes up the book and sits down with it before him and then deliberately drops ideas and symbols into his own subconscious mind, there to germinate until they are required. In the work of normal, ordinary reading, the memory and the mind may recollect the substance, may even be able to quote passages without difficulty; both these attributes have their uses, but they do not belong in the category of *creative* reading, and creative reading is part of the training of the mystery worker.

This method, however, is not for the young in the field; it has to be applied with discretion and discrimination and knowledge, or the last stage may be worse than the first; it is a form of highly trained selectivity, for the ideas and symbols need most careful consideration. It must be done when the heart and the subconscious mind and the spirit are all at one – when the union with the God is so established at the core that only those ideas and symbols which are suitable will be allowed to germinate; it is exemplified by the Egyptian affirmation 'I know Thee, Lord Tahuti, and Thou Me. I am Thou, and Thou art I'. It is the union in the mind representing the ploughed field in which the husbandman is scattering the seed for its germination, and unless it is applied with knowledge the seed may turn out to be tares and not ripe wheat. The parable of the sowing of the seed has a great deal in it which may be considered by the student who is about to seek out the teaching of the Mysteries.

The best way to read is to study the sacred books, poetry and even novels written by those who know something of the hidden knowledge and are trying to express it. The teaching of the Mysteries, being largely in the form of symbols, can often best be conveyed and concealed in fiction where the characters can be made to work out their problems in a manner which makes it easy for the average intelligent person to understand and appreciate them. There are many esoteric truths which it is easier and more suitable to convey under the guise of a story.

It must be remembered that the whole of the training in the Mysteries is intended to render the student more useful in the service of humanity. It is for this purpose, the development of the Divine Will on the plane of matter, for union with the Divine Will while still in incarnation, that the Mysteries are created; they are the outward and visible sign of man's eternal yearning to be at one with God.

To become a true worker in the Mysteries you must learn to decide first what form of religion is intended for you; then to use it practically by yourself and for yourself before you can hope to pass it on to others; if you cannot stand upon your own feet it will be a case of the halt leading the halt. And in using the word 'religion' in this place it should be understood in its widest sense as indicating that 'technique of adoration' which for you forms the link between the Seen and the Unseen, between the Higher and the Lower Worlds. It is literally the bond which links you to the Godhood.

Jesus taught this technique to His disciples in the upper room where only the initiates were permitted to sit with Him. He said 'I am come that ye might have life more abundantly'. Those who can understand the teaching and can tread the weary path which leads through the winding ways and ever up the hill will receive the vision from the summit; they will look out as Moses looked from Pisgah to see the promised land; they, too, will see before them the open plain and rising from it the City of Salvation that lies on the Hill of Vision. They too will be able to pass between the

Gates of Ivory and Horn which bar the way into the City and enter it as Princes and Rulers in Israel.

But before this goal is reached there is the unending struggle against the handicaps of this world. And one of the chief of these in the study of the Mysteries is Uncontrolled Fancy. To work the Mysteries successfully, the initiate must possess and use controlled imagination, for imagination is the jumping off board, so to speak, for the inner vision; it is the bridge which passes over the gulf between the real of the inner planes and the unreal of this world; which helps the incarnate to pass out of the confining realms of matter. Controlled imagination has been described as a clue to the phenomenon of genius; but uncontrolled fancies lead no-whither. They are the wandering stars, blown in the blackness of darkness for ever; comets, flaring across the sky and causing havoc by their blundering encounters; will-o'-the-wisps misleading travellers and plunging them into even greater difficulties, since it is always more simple to start from the beginning than to have to deal with the incubus of false knowledge and false symbolism. The writer must have his image clearly formed in his thoughts or he will not be able to convey it by the written word; the artist must have his conception clear before he puts the first line on the paper for his first draft, or his work will not be defined and intelligible to those who look at it. Even more must the student of the Mysteries have his imagination under full control.

The Age of Pisces has past from us and the Age of Aquarius is now ushered in. It is the age of the independent man, of the man who can bear his own burden, who is aware of the God Within and who knows his own purpose and his own goal. He is also the Water-carrier; the dispenser of the Water of Life. It is both our privilege and our duty to learn to co-operate as individuals working in groups of our own free will and accord. We must learn the independence which is our heritage and remember that in working the True Mysteries the hungry sheep never look up and are not fed. The Bread of Life is ours for the taking.

'Freely ye have received, freely give'. We have been given so much; we have so wonderful a history in these Islands of the Blessed; the Holy Land of the West. The lot has fallen to us in a fair ground and we have a goodly heritage. Let us then enter in and take seizin of our own.

Other titles from Thoth Publications

PRACTICAL MAGIC AND THE WESTERN MYSTERY TRADITION
Unpublished Essays and Articles by W. E. Butler.

W. E. Butler, a devoted friend and colleague of the celebrated occultist Dion Fortune, was among those who helped build the Society of the Inner Light into the foremost Mystery School of its day. He then went on to found his own school, the Servants of the Light, which still continues under the guidance of Dolores Ashcroft-Nowicki, herself an occultist and author of note and the editor and compiler of this volume.

PRACTICAL MAGIC AND THE WESTERN TRADITION is a collection of previously unpublished articles, training papers, and lectures covering many aspects of practical magic in the context of western occultism that show W. E. Butler not only as a leading figure in the magical tradition of the West, but also as one of its greatest teachers.

Subjects covered include:

What Makes an Occultist
Ritual Training
Inner Plane Contacts and Rays
The Witch Cult
Keys in Practical Magic
Telesmatic Images
Words of Power
An Explanation of Some Psychic Phenomena

ISBN 1-870450-32-9

THE CIRCUIT OF FORCE

by Dion Fortune.
With commentaries by Gareth Knight.

In "The Circuit of Force", Dion Fortune describes techniques for raising the personal magnetic forces within the human aura and their control and direction in magic and in life, which she regards as 'the Lost Secrets of the Western Esoteric Tradition'.

To recover these secrets she turns to three sources.

a) the Eastern Tradition of Hatha Yoga and Tantra and their teaching on raising the "sleeping serpent power" or kundalini;

b) the circle working by means of which spiritualist seances concentrate power for the manifestation of some of their results;

c) the linking up of cosmic and earth energies by means of the structured symbol patterns of the Qabalistic Tree of Life.

Originally produced for the instruction of members of her group, this is the first time that this material has been published for the general public in volume form.

Gareth Knight provides subject commentaries on various aspects of the etheric vehicle, filling in some of the practical details and implications that she left unsaid in the more secretive esoteric climate of the times in which she wrote.

Some quotes from Dion Fortune's text:

"When, in order to concentrate exclusively on God, we cut ourselves off from nature, we destroy our own roots. There must be in us a circuit between heaven and earth, not a one-way flow, draining us of all vitality. It is not enough that we draw up the Kundalini from the base of the spine; we must also draw down the divine light through the Thousand-Petalled Lotus. Equally, it is not enough for out mental health and spiritual development that we draw down the Divine Light, we must also draw up the earth forces. Only too often mental health is sacrificed to spiritual development through ignorance of, or denial of, this fact."

"....the clue to all these Mysteries is to be sought in the Tree of Life. Understand the significance of the Tree; arrange the symbols you are working with in the correct manner upon it, and all is clear and you can work out your sum. Equate the Danda with the Central Pillar, and the Lotuses with the Sephiroth and the bi-sections of the Paths thereon, and you have the necessary bilingual dictionary at your disposal - if you know how to use it."

ISBN 1-870450 28 0 Soft cover edition